ספר היראה
רבינו יונה

Sefer HaYirah
[The book of Awe]

Rabbeinu Yonah

לשון הקודש עם תרגום לאנגלית

Hebrew & English Translation

ידוע כי אין בר בלי תבן, כך אין ספר בלי טעויות, ועוד יודע אני כי דל ועני אני, **ואין עני אלא בדעה**. לכן מבקש אני בכל לשון של בקשה אם יש לכל אחד שאלות, הערות, הארות, תיקונים, נא לשלוח ל - simchatchaim@yahoo.com והשתדל לענות, ולתקן את הצריך תיקון.

אין לעשות שימוש כל שהוא בחומר שבחלק זה לצורך מסחרי, אלא רק ללמוד וללמד.
להשיג ספר זה או ספרים אחרים לאינפורמציה
simchatchaim@yahoo.com

Copyright © All Rights reserved to Itzhak Hoki Aboudi

כל הזכויות שמורות למהדיר © יצחק חוגי עבודי

מהדורה ראשונה תשפ"ד 2023

Sefer HaYirah   ספר היראה

Content of the book   תוכן הספר

דף Page	תוכן Content
2.	רבינו יונה וספר היראה Rabbi Yonah Gerondi and Sefer HaYirah
5.	הקדמה Introduction
8.	כל בוקר Every morning
20.	בית הכנסת Synagogue
27.	תפילת העמידה Prayer of 18
34.	אחרי בית הכנסת After the synagogue
40.	עסקים Business
45.	בבית ואורחים At home and guests
49.	עם אנשים With people
57.	כבוד אב ואם וחכם Honor father and mother and sag
62.	עזרה לזולת Helping Others
65.	דבור נקי Clean speech
73.	נשים Women
78.	בדרך On the way
90.	לעת ערב In the evening
95.	שבת Sabbath
100.	חגים Holidays

Sefer HaYirah ספר היראה

רבינו יונה וספר היראה

רבי יונה גירונדי המכונה **רבנו יונה**, נולד סביב שנת ד'תתק"ע – 1210 והסתלק בכ"ח בחשוון ה'כ"ד 1263, ידוע גם בשם **החסיד**, בן רבי אברהם שהיה רב מתקופת הראשונים, מחבר הספר **שערי תשובה**. בצעירותו למד אצל רבי שלמה מן ההר מונטפלייר, ואצל האחים רבי משה בר שניאור ורבי שמואל בר שניאור. למד גם מבן דודו הרמב"ן, אימו של הרמב"ן היא אחותו של רבי אברהם, אביו של רבנו יונה, והתקשר עמו בקשרי חיתון, כאשר השיא את בתו לרבי שלמה, בנו של הרמב"ן. בשנת 1244 מונה לרב בטולדו. היה רבו של הרשב"א.

רבנו יונה נודע כבעל חריפות ועוצמה למדנית גדולה מאוד בעולם התלמודי, וכתב חידושים לכמה מסכתות. אך כיום נשאר רק חידושיו למסכת בבא בתרא הנקרא בשם - עליות דרבנו יונה. בחיבור עצמו מעלה רבנו יונה דיונים מעמיקים על סדר המסכת, סוגיה אחר סוגיה. בסוף כל דיון מביא רבנו יונה את מה **שעלה בידנו**, הכוונה היא לפרטים אותם פוסק רבנו יונה להלכה, ומכאן גם שמו של החיבור.

ספר היראה הוא אחד מספרי המוסר החשובים של רבי יונה גירונדי בעל הספר **שערי תשובה**, אשר ספריו התפשטו בכל תפוצות ישראל.

ספר היראה הוא ספר קצר יחסית, ולכן אינו מחולק לפרקים. הוא סוקר את מאורעות יומו של היהודי, החל **מהקיצו משנתו** עד **בשוכבו על מיטתו בלילה**. בסוף הספר מביא גם מעט עניינים על השבת, ועל מועדי ישראל. לרוב, הבית יוסף והבית חדש מציינים את דברי רבינו יונה בעיקר מספר זה עקב היותו עוסק בענייני אורח חיים, **בספר היראה** כמקור לפסקיו של רבי יעקב בן רבי אשר בספרו **הטור**, וכן הגר"א בביאורו לשולחן ערוך, מציין הרבה את דברי רבינו בספר היראה כמקור לפסקי השולחן ערוך. למעשה, ספר היראה הוא ייישומו המעשי של הספר שערי תשובה.

Sefer HaYirah   ספר היראה

Rabbi Yonah Gerondi and Sefer HaYirah

Rabbi Yonah Gerondi, known as **Rabbeinu Yonah**, was born around the year 1210 - and passed away on the 24th of Cheshvan 1263, also known as **The Hasid**, son of Rabbi Avraham who was a rabbi from the Rishonim period, author of the book **Shaarei Teshuvah**.

In his youth he studied with Rabbi Shlomo of Mount Montpellier, and with the brothers Rabbi Moshe Bar Shneur and Rabbi Shmuel Bar Shneur. He also learned from his cousin the Ramban. The mother of the Ramban was the sister of Rabbi Avraham, the father of our Rabbi Yonah, and him were related through marriage when he married his daughter to Rabbi Shlomo, the son of the Ramban. In 1244 he was appointed rabbi in the city of Toledo.

Rabbeinu Yonah was known to have a very great scholarly sharpness and power in the Talmudic world, and he wrote innovations for several treatises. But today only his innovations remain for the parts in the Talmud Bava Batra. They are called the - Aliyot Darbnu Yonah. In the essay itself, Rabbeinu Yonah raises in-depth the discussions on the order of the Talmud, issue after issue. At the end of each discussion, Rabbeinu Yonah brings what we have come up with, referring to the details that Rabbeinu Yonah rules according to Halacha, hence the name of the essay.

The **Book of Yirah** [The book of Awe] is one of the important moral books of Rabbi Yonah Gerondi, author of the book **Shaarei Teshuvah**, whose books have spread throughout the Diaspora of Israel.

The **Book of Yirah** is a relatively short book, and therefore is not divided into chapters. He reviews the day's events of every Jew, from waking up from his sleep to lying on his bed

Sefer HaYirah   ספר היראה

at night. At the end of the book, he also brings a few matters about the Sabbath, and the Holidays of Israel.

Most of the time, Beit Yosef and the HaBach mentions the words of Rabbeinu Yonah, mainly from this book due to his dealing with lifestyle matters, in the **Book of Yirah**, as a source for the rulings of Rabbi Yaakov ben Rabbi Asher in his **TOR**, and the **HaGra** [Rabbi Eliyahu from Vilna] in his commentary on **Shulchan Aruch**.

In fact, the Book of Yirah is the practical application of the book **Shaarei Teshuvah**.

Sefer HaYirah

ספר היראה
Sefer HaYirah

הקדמה introduction

להורות לעם ה' את דרך ה', ואת המעשה אשר יעשון כל ימיהם, בשבתם ובקומם, בלכתם ובבואם, למען ייטב להם ולבניהם, בזה ובבא.

טוב[1] לגבר כי ישא על בנעוריו. כי טוב לאדם לשאת ולסבול עולו של הקדוש ברוך הוא ולתת מוסרות ומוטות על צווארו, להיכנס לעבודת בורא העולם.

It is good that a man should take up the Yoke - of the commandments in his youth. For it is good that a person should take up and to endure the Yoke of the Holy One Blessed Be He and to set the reins and the staffs upon his neck to enter into the service of the Creator of the World.

ויזכור[2] את בוראו בימי בחורותיו.

Now he should remember his Creator in the days of his youth.

ובכל יום ויום יוסיף אומץ ויתחזק במצות בורא עולם.

Each and every day he should strengthen and be encouraged in the commandments of the Creator of the World.

ויכניס אהבתו בליבו.

---

[1] איכה ג כז
[2] מלשון הכתוב - וזכור את בוראיך בימי בחורותיך [קהלת יב א]

Sefer HaYirah   ספר היראה

He should bring His love into his heart.

ויחשוב הבורא תמיד לנגד עיניו, ועל ידי כן ייתן יראת הצור על פניו.

And he should think of his Creator as eternally before his very eyes. And thus, he may set the fear of the Rock **of Israel** upon his face.

ויכניע לבו.

And make his heart tremble.

וישפיל קומתו ואת רום עיניו.

And lower his spirits and lower his stature and the height of his eyes.

וילך שחוח, ויתהה על עוונות נעוריו.

Let him go along bent over, regretting the sins of his youth.

ויבכה עליהם תמיד.

And always crying over them.

וישמור בכל כוחו מחטוא עוד במסתרים, ולא יעשה במחשך מעשיו, ואז יהיה אהוב ונחמד בעיני הבורא, וכל רואיו יאשרוהו.

So let him keep with all his strength from sinning more in secret, and let him not do it in dark deeds. And so he will be beloved and treasured in the eyes of the Creator and all who see him will rejoice in him.

אלה הדברים אשר יעשה אותם האדם וחי בהם חיי

Sefer HaYirah ספר היראה

העולם.
These are the things that a man may do and live life everlasting by them.

Sefer HaYirah ספר היראה

בכל בוקר Every morning

בכל בוקר בהקיצו משנתו:
Every morning when he awakens from his sleep.

בכל בוקר בהקיצו משנתו, יזדעזע ויהיה נרתע ונחפז מאימת הבורא בזכרו חסדו אשר עשה לו ואמונתו אשר שמר לו, כי החזיר לו נשמתו אשר הפקיד אצלו.
Every morning when he awakens from his sleep, let him tremble and be startled and seized by the fear of the Creator when he remembers the loving kindness by which He did for him and the faith which He kept by him, for He returned his soul which He entrusted to him.

ואז יברך בליבו את הבורא, אשר הגדיל לעשות עמו, כי חידש והחליף כוחו. ובשומו הדברים האלה אל לבו, תבער אהבת הבורא בליבו.
So then with all his heart let him bless the Creator who has done great things with him, for He has renewed and restored his strength. And when he sets these words upon his heart the love of the Creator will burn in his heart.

ואז אל ייסוב על מיטתו דרך עצל, אך במהירות וזריזות יקום מיד. ואם יפגע בו מנוול ויוליכנו דרך עצלות, ישיב אמריו לו וישים אל לבו, כי אם יקרא בעל-חוב או אדם אחר אליו, יקום מיד, או מפני כבוד אדם, או מפני ריווח שיביא לו חיי שעה, או מיראת הפסד ממון, כמו נפלה דלקה בעיר, יקום מיד במהרה ולא יתרשל. או אם יצטרך ללכת לעבודת המלך, יקום ואל יתרשל פן יעלילו עליו. או

ספר היראה | Sefer HaYirah

למצוא חן בעיני המלך. על אחת כמה וכמה לעבודת מלך מלכי המלכים הקדוש ברוך הוא, שיש לו להיזהר לקום במהירות ובזריזות, וייירא פן יאחר לבוא.

So then, he should not roll over upon his bed in the way of a sluggard, but rather with speed and vigor let him rise immediately. But if he be disfigured by plague and it should cause him to go about in a lazy way, let him reply His words to him and pay attention to it, for if a creditor whether gentile or another man – shall call after him, he should rise immediately, whether because of the honor due to the man, whether because of the momentary gain that it shall bring to him, or from fear of financial loss, like falling on the fuel of the fire, let him get up immediately, speedily, and not be lax. Or, if he needs to go to the service of the prince let him get up and not be lax. Otherwise, they may heap abuse upon him. Or just to find favor in the eyes of the prince. How much the more so in the service of the King of Kings of Kings, the Holy One Blessed be He, so he must take heed to rise with speed, vigorousness, and awe, else he may be late to come. And how good and pleasant it is if he should rise before the light of the morning to supplicate himself before his Creator and to direct the hours of the different night-watches dividing the night into three equal parts, since these are the times the Holy One is reminded of the destruction of the Temple and the exile of Israel among the nations and the prayer that a man may pray at

Sefer HaYirah

that hour about the destruction and the exile is desired and his supplication falls before the Omnipresent One, whether he lengthens or shortens his prayers so long as he directs his heart with his supplications, for better to say little with intention than much without intention.

וכל מעשיו יחשוב לעשות לשם שמים, ולפי כוחו ילך בדרכי החכמים, ויהיה נכנע.

Now, he should think to do all of his deeds for the sake of Heaven. And he should, as much as he is able, go by the way of the sages. But let him be humble.

אל יעמוד ערום ממיטתו, אף מיושב, כמו שהיה מתפאר רבי יוסי - מימי[3] לא ראו קורות ביתי אמרי חלוקי. אך ייקח חלוקו ויכניס בו ראשו וזרועות, ואז בקומו יהיה מכוסה. ואל יאמר, הנני בחדרי חדרים בבית אפל, מי רואני ומי מעידני, כי - מלוא[4] כל הארץ כבודו. לפניו - כחשכה[5] כאורה.

Let him not get out of bed naked but only sit up. As Rabbi Yossi explained -In all my life the inside of my tunic did not see the beams of my house. Instead, let him take his undershirt and put his head and arms in it, so that when he gets up, he will be covered. And he should not say, "Why, here I am in the inner rooms of a dark house, who will see me and who will know it is

---

[3] שבת קיח ב
[4] ישעיהו ו ג
[5] תהלים קלט יב

Sefer HaYirah / ספר היראה

me?" for the whole earth is full of His glory. Before Him, the darkness is like light.

וילבש בגדיו, ויהיה לו טלית קטן וילבשנו מתחת למדיו, כי עקר מצות ציצית לזיכרון ללבשו תמיד, כי לזיכרון המצות נתנה, ולמען לא יסור האדם אחרי שרירות לבו ואחרי מראה עיניו המחטיאות את הגוף. והדרך הזה לא ימצא כי אם בלכתו בדרך אשר דברי ערווה מצויים שם.

Now he should put on his clothes. He should have a tallit katan and let him put it on underneath his outer garments for the crux of the commandment of wearing fringes is always remembering when getting dressed. Because the commandment was given for remembering, and so that a man should not turn away after the stubbornness of his heart or after the gaze of his eyes which cause his body to sin. But this way will not be found unless he should go on the way in which the naked things are found.

על כן ילבש אותו מיד בלא ברכה אם לא רחץ ידיו. וטוב להיות זריז ליטול ידיו קודם ויברך עובר לעשייתו.

Therefore, let him dress himself immediately without a blessing if he has not washed his hands. But it is good to be strict to wash his hands first and to bless after he has done it.

וצריך להתעטף [בציצית] מעומד.

Now it is necessary to wrap himself in a tallit in a standing position.

Sefer HaYirah ספר הירא**ה**

ואותו טלית קטן, טוב שיהיה כעין סרבל, כי אין בזה פקפוק.

And it is good for that same tallit katan to be a kind of cloak for there is no shaking with this.

וינעל מנעליו, של ימין תחלה ואחר כך של שמאל, ויקשור של שמאל ואחר כך של ימין, כמו שאמרו רבותינו - ירא[6] שמים יוצא ידי שתיהן, לקיים דברי שתיהן. לקיים דברי המשנה ודברי רבי יוחנן, כתפיליו כך מנעליו, מה תפיליו בשמאל, אף מנעליו בשמאל.

Now let him put on his right shoe first and the left one afterwards but tie the left one first and afterwards the right, as our rabbis said, "Awe of heaven coming out of all of them," to fulfill the words of the Mishnah and the words of Rabbi Yochanan - just as his prayers, thus his shoes - just as his prayers on the left, so his shoes on the left.

ומעת קומו להתהלך על הדרך, יכפוף קומתו וישוח ראשו, כי השכינה למעלה מראשו.

And as soon as he gets up to walk on the road, he should bend his height and he should cover his head for the **Shekhinah** [The presence of God] is above his head.

ולכן נכון לכסות ראשו, ואל יהיה בגילוי ראש.

And therefore, it is correct to cover his head and not to go bareheaded.

וילך ויבדוק עצמו בבית הכסא.

---

[6] שבת סא א

Sefer HaYirah   ספר היראה

Now, let a man go and let him take care of his needs in the bathroom.

ושם יהיה צנוע, אל יגלה עצמו כי אם לפניו טפח ומאחוריו טפחים, והאישה מלאחריה טפח ומלפניה ולא כלום.

And there he should be modest. He should not expose himself but for a hands-breadth in front of him and two hands-breadths behind him. And for a woman, one hands-breadth behind her and in front of her, nothing.

ולא ישתין מעומד, פן יהיו ניצוצות נתזים על רגליו ויראה ככרות שפכה, אלא יעמוד במקום גבוה או ישתין בעפר תחוח. ואם ישתין מעומד, יזהר פן יאחוז באמה, אלא מעטרה ולמטה לצד הארץ. ואף אם הוא נשוי, כי אחרי אשר העונש גדול כל כך שהוא מביא מבול לעולם, מאוד יש לו לאדם להתחזק ולקדש עצמו אף במותר לו. וכן - רבנו[7] הקדוש מימיו לא הכניס ידיו למטה מאבנטו.

He should not urinate standing up in case there be sprinkles splashing upon his legs and he should appear like one whose urinary canal is mutilated. Rather, let him stand in a high place or urinate in dust. But if he does urinate standing up, he should take care lest he take hold of the membrum virile rather, he should hold it from the corona on down the lower side even if he be married. For the punishment for it is so great as to destroy the world. He must strengthen himself and sanctify himself, even in what is permitted to him. And thus, our holy Rabbi - in all his days he did not put his hand

---

[7] שבת קיח ב

Sefer HaYirah   ספר הירא‎ה

under his belt.

וכשישב לפנות, ישב ויגלה, ויכסה ויקום.
When he sits to relieve himself, he shall sit and uncover and cover and stand.

ואל יפציר עצמו לפנות בחוזק, פן ינתקו שני הכרכשתא ויסתכן.
But he should not strain himself hard in case he should tear the glands of the rectum and be in danger.

ויקנח בשמאל אבל לא בימין. מפני שמראה בה טעמי תורה ואוכל בה.
But he should not strain himself hard in case he should tear the glands of the rectum and be in danger.

ויבדוק עצמו יפה יפה, כי אחרי אשר קרביו ובני-מעיו צריכים לברך את הבורא תמיד שנאמר - ברכי[8] נפשי את הוי"ה וכל קרבי את שם קדשו, אין נאה להביא בטן מלאה צואה לפני הקדוש ברוך הוא, ריבונו של עולם לברכו.
He should inspect himself very well afterwards for his guts and his bowels need to bless the Creator always, as is said - Bless the ETERNAL, O my soul, and all my innards His holy name," It is not fitting to bring a belly full of excrement before the Holy One, Blessed be He, Master of the Universe, to bless Him.

וישמור פן ילכלך בגדיו לא במי רגלים ולא ברעי.

---

[8] תהילים קג א

Sefer HaYirah ספר היראה

Let him take care lest he soil his clothes, whether with urine or with excrement.

אם יש לו יכולת, יהיו לו שני מכנסים. אחד, שלובש בשעת התפלה לבד, למען יהיה נקי יותר בתפלתו. ואם אין לו, יזהר שלא יטנף את שלו.

If he can, he should have two pairs of pants one that he wears at the time of prayer only for the sake of being the most clean when praying, but if he cannot, he should be careful not to soil his pants.

ויכבסם תמיד להסיר כתמי-הצואה מעליהן.

He should always wash them to take away the stains of filth from off of them.

וירחץ בניקיון כפיו במים אם יש לו. ירחצם יפה יפה, ויברך עליהם **על נטילת ידים**.

He should wash his hands completely. with water if he has it. He should wash them exceedingly well and recite the al **Netilat Yadayim** [Washing hands], Concerning the washing of the hands. blessing over them.

ובברכת **אשר יצר**, ימתין עד התפלה. ואם ברך **אשר יצר**, יאמר עמה - **אלה"י נשמה שנתת בי**, כי היא סמוכה לה, ולפיכך אינה פותחת בברוך. ואז בעת התפלה יתחיל - **אשר נתן לשכווי בינה**.

He should wait until prayer to recite the – **Asher Yatzar** blessing [said after going to the washroom], but if he does say Asher Yatzar, he should also say the blessing that begins **Elohai**

Sefer HaYirah   ספר היראה

Neshamah [My God, the soul that you breathed into me is pure] with it for it is dependent upon it and therefore it does not begin with **Baruch** [blessed be] so at the time of praying he should begin …who has given the rooster knowledge.

או יחזור ויברך **אשר יצר**.
Or then he should go back and repeat Asher Yatzar.

ועל **נטילת ידים** יברך בשעת ניגוב, ולא בנטילתן.
He should recite the - **Al Netilat Yadayim** [blessing after washing your hands upon waking up in the morning] the blessing is said when he dries his hands, not when he washes them.

ומיד יברך **על מצות ציצית** בטלית אשר לבש, אם לא ברך בהתעטפו.
Then he should immediately recite the "…about the mitzvah of fringes" blessing on the Tallit which he put on if he did not bless when he wrapped himself.

ובכל פעם שהוא מתעטף, צריך לברך.
But every time that he wraps himself, he needs to recite the blessing.

ואחרי כן יניח תפלה של יד בזרוע שמאל למעלה מן הפרק שקורין קובדו בלע"ז ממש כנגד הלב, ויברך **להניח תפילין**.

Sefer HaYirah ספר היראה

Then afterwards he should lay the arm-tefillin on the left arm above the part that they call the elbow in the common tongue, adjusted slightly toward the heart and recite the blessing, …**To Lay Tefillin**. After that he should put on the head-tefillin next to the brain and recite the …about the commandment of tefillin blessing.

ואחר כך ישים של ראש כנגד המוח ויברך **על מצות תפילין**. ואל ידבר בין תפלה של יד לתפלה של ראש. שח בין תפלה לתפלה - חוזר ומברך על של ראש שתים, **להניח ועל מצות**.

He should not speak between the arm-tefillin and the head-tefillin. if one chats between the tefillin he should go back and bless over the head-piece twice, …**To Lay**… and …**About the Mitzvah of Tefillin**…

ותמיד ימשמש בתפילין, בשל יד ואחר כך בשל ראש, למען יזהר להיות בנקיות, כי תפילין צריכין גוף נקי, שלא יפיח בהן, ושלא יישן בהן.

He should always handle the arm-tefillin first and the head-tefillin afterwards so that he shall be careful to be clean for tefillin require a clean body that shall not fart in them and shall not sleep in them.

וצריך לברך כשימשמש זמן גדול אחר הנחתן, דקיימא[9] לן כרבנן דבי רב אשי - דכל אימת דממשמשי בהו מברכי.

And he needs to bless when he handles them for a long time after putting them on, as it is

---

[9] סוכה מו א

Sefer HaYirah — ספר היראה

established according to the Rabbis in the name of Rabbi Ashi - every time I handled them, I blessed them.

ומפי מורי הרב רבי שמואל ברבי שניאור שמעתי, דאין צריך לברך משום משמוש, אלא כשהן נעקרות ממקומן, והוא מחזירן למקומן.

But according to my teacher Rabbi Shmuel bar Shneur I heard that one does not need to bless on account of handling except when they are taken out from their place and he returns them to their place.

ולעניין שינה, יש שלשה חלוקים בדבר -

Now, with regard to the matter of sleep there are three parts to the matter -

א. כשהן בראשו, יישן בהן שנת עראי אבל לא קבע.

A. When they are on his head, he may nap but not sleep.

ב. וכשהוא אוחזן בידו, לא עראי ולא קבע, פן יפלו מידו.

B. But when they are held in his hand he may not sleep or nap in case they fall from his hand.

ג. ואם הניחן אצל מראשותיו, יפרוש סודר עליהן ויישן אצלן בין עראי ובין קבע.

C. Now if he puts them on where he lies down let him spread a blanket over them and sleep. And in them he may sleep something between a nap and a full sleep.

Sefer HaYirah / ספר היראה

וכשנכנס לבית הכסא, חולצן חוץ לארבע אמות, או כורכן ומניחן בכלי תוך כלי בחיקו כנגד לבו.

When he goes to the bathroom, he takes them off outside the four cubits [of the bathroom] or winds them up and sets them down in a vessel inside a vessel in his pocket next to his heart.

Sefer HaYirah   ספר היראה

בית הכנסת synagogue

וילך לבית הכנסת. ובבואו סמוך לבית-הכנסת, ימהר פעמיו, כמו שכתוב - בבית[10] אלוהים נהלך ברגש.

Then he should go to the synagogue. And when he comes close to the synagogue he should quicken his steps, as is written - In the house of God let us walk in excitement.

ויבדוק מנעליו פן יהיו מטונפים, וכן אמר שלמה בחכמתו - שמור[11] רגליך כאשר תלך אל בית האלהים.

But he should check his shoes in case they are filthy or soiled as King Solomon said in his Wisdom - Guard your foot when you go to the house of God.

ויבוא לבית הכנסת, ואומר בכניסתו - ואני[12] ברב חסדך אבוא ביתך אשתחווה אל היכל קודשך ביראתך. וישב במקומו.

He should come to the synagogue and speak when he enters - As for me, in your great love I shall come to your house, I shall bow down to your holy temple in fear of You. and he should sit in his seat.

ואם יש לו עוד טלית, יתכסה בו ויברך **להתעטף בציצית**.

If he has another tallis he should cover himself in it and recite the blessing - to wrap oneself in tzitzit.

---

[10] תהילים נה טו
[11] קהלת ד יז
[12] תהילים ה ח

Sefer HaYirah　　ספר הירְאָה.

וישב, ולא יפתח פיו עד שישהה מעט, וישים אל לבו לפני מי הוא עומד, ומי השומע דבריו. ואז ילבש חרדה ואימה וזיע ורתת.

Then he should sit and not open his mouth until he pauses a little and answers in his heart. Before Whom he stands and Who is the One hearing his words. And thus, he will be seized by trembling, fear, sweating, and feeling awestruck.

ויפתח תפלתו על הסדר - אחד[13] המרבה ואחד הממעיט ובלבד שיכוון לבו לשמים.

Now let him begin his prayer in the proper order, it does not matter whether one that lengthens or one that shortens, only that so long as he directs his heart to heaven.

ויתקן מלבושיו, שנאמר - היכון[14] לקראת אלוהיך ישראל.

He should prepare his clothes, as is said - Prepare to meet your God, Israel.

וכשהוא מתפלל, אל יגביה קולו בתפלתו.

And when he prays, he should not raise his voice in his prayer.

אך ישמיע לאוזניו מה שיוציא מפיו.

But he should speak only loud enough so that his own ears hear what comes out of his mouth.

ויחתוך בשפתיו כל תיבה ותיבה, ואל יבלען. גם סוף התיבות יחתוך להפרידן מהתיבה הסמוכה להן, פן ייכשל

---

[13] ברכות ה ב
[14] עמוס ד יב

Sefer HaYirah   ספר הַיִרְאָה

בספרו בגויים את-כבודו, שבחי ירושלים את ה', וכן כל **את, ואותו, ואותה,** הסמוכות למ"ם, צריך להפרידן זו מזו, וכן **אלוהיכם אמת**, וכיוצא באלה.

He should clearly enunciate each and every letter. He should not swallow them. Also, he should enunciate the end of the words to separate them from the word next to it in case he stumbles over - tell of His glory among the gentiles. Or - praises of Jerusalem. And so, it is with each and every et, **Ve'otoh, Ve'otah**. that is next to a letter man one needs to separate them, this one from that one, and so with Adonai **Elocheichem Emet** [Your God is the truth] and such as come out with these.

ולא יהיה מאריך בתפלתו יותר מדי בצבור, פן יחשבוהו ליהיר ולץ.

He should not be one who lengthens his prayer too much in public in case they should think him a show-off or a scoffer.

ובקריאת שמע יהיה מאוד נזהר שיוציא בשפתיו וישמיע לאוזניו מאתים וארבעים ושמונה תיבות שבו.

When he recites the **Sh'ma** he should be very careful to utter with his lips and hear with his ears all 248 letters that are in it.

וייתן ריווח בין הדבקים, כדברי רבותינו[15] - בכל-לבבך, ועל-לבבך, וכיוצא בהן.

But he must allow an interval between words that may easily run into one another. According

---

[15] ברכות טו ב

Sefer HaYirah / ספר היראה

to the words of our Rabbis, peace be upon them - **With All of Your Heart**, and - **Upon Your Heart**, and such like them.

ובכל אחד ואחד משלשה שמות האמורים בפסוק ראשון, יאריך עד שיחשוב - **היה הווה יהיה**. ולא יאריך ב**אל"ף** דאחד.

And with each and every One of the three divine names that are in the first line he should lengthen them until he thinks of past, present, and future but he should not lengthen the Aleph **One**.

ולא ימהר ב**ח**' לקרותה בחטף.

And he should not hurry the letter **Chet**, in the word **Echad**, as if to read it with a **Chataf**.

ויאריך ב**דל"ת**, עד שיחשוב בלבבו שבורא עולם הוא מלך למעלה ולמטה בשמים ובארץ, ובארבע רוחות העולם ממזרח וממערב מצפון ומדרום ותהום רבה, ומאתים וארבעים ושמונה אברים שבו.

And he should lengthen the letter **Dalet** in the word **Echad**, until he considers in his heart that the Creator of the world is king above and below, in heaven and on earth, and the four winds of the world, from east and the west, north and south, and the great depth, and the 248 limbs that are in him.

ואם לא יוכל לכוון כל כך, יכוון השם שהוא עתה אלוהינו, עתיד להיות אחד.

But if he just cannot direct his heart so much

Sefer HaYirah ספר היראה

have so much **Kavvanah** [Intention] let him direct himself to Hashem, who is now our God, in the future to be one.

ובכל פעם בהזכירו שם המיוחד יחשוב בו פירוש קריאתו שהוא אדון כל.

And each time he mentions the Specific Name of GOD let him think on it the meaning of its reading: that He is Lord of all.

בכל[16] לבבך, בשני יצריך, יצר טוב ויצר רע. ובכל נפשך, אפילו נוטל נשמתך. ובכל מאודך, בכל מידה ומידה שהוא מודד לך.

When he recites - **With all your heart**. he will need to meditate on two things: The good appetite and the evil appetite. When he recites - **And with all your soul**. is even taking your soul. When he recites - **And with all your might**. means Whatever measure that He measured out for you.

אשר[17] אנכי מצוך היום. יפסיק עד יחשוב היום נצטוו לי.

At - **Which I command you today**. let him pause and consider - today they were commanded to me.

על לבבך. עד כאן כוונת הלב, ועיקר קבלת על מלכות שמים. ואפילו מהלך בדרך, נכון לעמוד עד שיגיע **על לבבך**.

Upon your heart. thus far, the intention of the heart and the crux of the acceptance of the

---

[16] משנה ברכות ט ה
[17] דברים ו ו

Sefer HaYirah ספר היראה

Yoke of the kingdom of heaven, and even when walking on the road, being directed until he arrives at - **Upon your heart**.

אך מפסוק ראשון יצא ידי חובה.
But even from the first verse, he has fulfilled his obligation.

מכאן ואילך יקרא כדרכו בכוונה לפי כוחו.
From here on he should read according to his usual way with as much intention as he can.

כשיגיע ל-וקשרתם[18] לאות על ידך. ימשמש בתפילין של יד. ל-והיו לטוטפות בין עיניך. ימשמש בתפילין של ראש.
And for when he arrives at - **Bind them for a sign upon your hand**, he should touch the arm tefillin. And for when he arrives at - **For totafot between your eyes**, he should touch that of the head.

וכשיגיע ל-וראיתם[19] אותו. יעיין בציציתו.
And when he comes to - **And look at it**. he should look at his tzitzit.

ויחתוך זי"ן ד**תזכרו**.
Plus, he should enunciate the letter **zayin** [זּ] in the word - **Tizkaru**, you shall remember.

ואל ירמוז בעיניו ויקרוץ בשפתיו וימלול ברגליו ויורה

---

[18] דברים ו ח
[19] במדבר טו לט

Sefer HaYirah ספר היראה

באצבעותיו, כי - תועבת[20] ה' כל עושה אלה.

And he should not wink, nor gesticulate with his lips, or one who rubs his legs, or one who points with his fingers. **For anyone who does these is an abomination of the LORD.**

---

[20] דברים כה טז

Sefer HaYirah   ספר הירְאָה

תפילת העמידה Prayer of 18

ובתפלתו מיושב אל יסמוך לאחריו, ולא יהא נוטה לצדדין דרך גאווה, אלא ישב וראשו כפוף, שלא יראה פני היושב כנגדו חוץ לארבע אמותיו. ושני אציליו על עצם הירך מקום חיבורו לגוף מכאן ומכאן.

Now, one who sits in prayer should not lean on something behind him, nor shall he lean to his sides in the manner of a proud person. Rather, he should sit with his head bowed so that he should not see the face of the person sitting in front of him beyond his four cubits. And his arms aligned with the body, with hands crossed over the waist.

ושתי ידיו תחת לבושו, הימנית על השמאלית כנגד טבורו. ואל יפשוט רגליו, אך יהיו שוקיו על עומדן, למען יהיה יותר ברעדה וביראה.

And his two hands should be under his clothes, the right over the left in front of his navel and he should not stretch his legs but rather sit upright upon his **sit** bones in order that he should be more trembling and fearful.

וינענע כל גופו, לקיים - כל[21] עצמתי תאמרנה.

Then he should shake his body like a lulav to fulfill the verse - **All my bones shall say, LORD**…

ובקומו להתפלל, יכוון רגליו זו אצל זו.

When he stands up to pray, he should stand

---

[21] תהילים לה י

Sefer HaYirah / ספר היראה

with his legs next to one another.

וישוח ראשו.
He should bow his head.

וידחוק אצילױ לגופו נגד חגורתו, וישים ידיו תחת לבושו, הימנית על השמאלית.
Let him press his elbows into his body until his belt, and let him place his hands below his clothing, the right over the left.

ועושה שבע כריעות.
He makes seven bows.

ישחה בברכת **אבות** תחילה וסוף.
He shall bend at the beginning and end of the **Avot** [The first section of the Amidah]

ישחה ב**ברוך אתה** במהירות ויזקוף בשם ה' בנחת, וישחה ב**מודים** תחלה וסוף, ולא יותר בברכות.
He should bow quickly at **You are blessed**, and he should straighten up slowly at the divine Name **'ה**. he should bow at the beginning and the end of the **Modim** [thanksgiving section of the Amidah] and no more in the eighteen benedictions of the Amidah.

אבל כשהוא פוסע שלש פסיעות, נותן שלום בשמאל בתחילה וכורע, לימין וכורע, לפניו וכורע.
But when he takes three steps, he gives peace beginning with the left, to the right and bows, before him and bows.

Sefer HaYirah   ספר היראה

ותהיה הכריעה כמו שאמרו חכמים - עד[22] שיתפקקו כל חוליות שבשדרה, ועד כדי שייראה איסר כנגד לבו, וזהו בשר ברוחב איסר בין פרק חוליות השדרה כנגד הלב. וכשאדם זקוף, מובלע ואינו נראה. וכשהוא שוחה, אז יתפרדו החוליות ונראה אותו-בשר.

The bow should be as the sages said, until all the vertebrae in the spine shall protrude until he is able to see an **Isar** [Old Jewish coin from the of the Temple] of flesh opposite his heart now this is fleshing the width of an **Isar** between the part of the spine opposite the heart. And when the person straightens, it disappears and is not seen. And when he bows, the vertebrae of the spine separate themselves and the same flesh reappears.

ואל יחזור מיד למקומו, פן ייחשב ככלב שב על קיאו.
He should not immediately return to his place lest he be thought like a dog returning to its vomit.

ולא יירק בתפלתו. ואם נזדמן לו רוק, מבליעו בכסותו.
He should not spit during his prayer. But if he is spat upon, he hides the spittle in his cloak.

ואף לא יגהק, ולא יפהק. ואם פיהק, מניח ידו על סנטרו או על פיו.
He should not even belch or yawn, but if he does yawn, he puts his hand upon his chin or over his mouth.

---

[22] ברכות כח ב

Sefer HaYirah ספר היראה

ולא יאחז מאומה בידו, כי יירא פן ייפול מידו ולא יתכוון.
He should not hold anything at all in his hand, for he should be afraid lest it fall from his hand and he will not be deliberate in his prayer.

ולא יתפלל לא כנגד רבו, ולא לאחורי רבו.
Neither in front of nor behind his master shall he pray.

ויסדר תפלתו.
He should offer praise in his prayer.

אך לא יעשנה קבע כאדם האומר חוק קבוע הוא עלי בכל יום, כך וכך תפלות מוטלות חובה עלי. אלא יעשנה תחנונים לפני המקום.
But he should not make it fixed like the person who says, it is a fixed law upon me every day, the obligation to say such and such prayers lies upon me, but rather let him make them supplications before the Omnipresent One.

ואל יעיין בתפלתו לאמור, כמה התפללתי בכוונה, ראויה היא להתקבל, כי הוא משלושה דברים המזכירים עונותיו של אדם, כי מקטרגים עליו ואומרים, וכי ראוי הוא לכך שתתקבל תפלתו, והלא עשה כך וכך. אך יחשוב בלבבו, כי מאוד היה לו לעמוד בתפלה יותר, אולי יכפר אחד מעונותיו הקטנים, ויזכור כי בשר הוא, רוח הולך ולא ישוב.
Let him not contemplate his prayer, saying, I have prayed so much with intentionality, it is worthy to be accepted, for it is one of three things mentioned in connection with the sins of

Sefer HaYirah ספר היראה

a person for they accuse him about them, saying, "Is it worthy that such a prayer should be accepted, and has he not done such and such?" But let him think in his heart that he really should have stood much longer in prayer, perhaps one of his smaller sins would be forgiven, and let him remember that is he is but flesh and blood, breath leaving and not returning.

ומה יתרון לו להתגאות במעשיו, הלא לכך נוצר. ואם על כורחו יגאה לבו, ישים אל לבו גאוני עולם שגוועו ועברו מן העולם אשר עשו טובה אלף ידות יותר ממנו.

And what gain is there for him to boast about his deeds? Should he not be on guard for such as this? But if his heart must grow proud, let him think about great people of the world that fell away and passed away from the world but which did a thousand times better than he.

ובעודו בבית הכנסת, אל ידבר דיבור חול עם אדם, ואף כי בשעת קריאת התורה.

Now, while he is still in the synagogue, let him not speak a profane word with a person, especially not during the reading of the Torah.

ואם ישבו אצלו בני אדם המדברים, יניע שפתיו וידמה עצמו כמתפלל, ואל יתפאר לומר - **איני מדבר**, כי כל המתפאר כמעט הוא נוטל את שכרו.

But if some people sat by him talking intentionally let him shake his lips in disdain and make himself quiet as when he prays. But

Sefer HaYirah ספר היראה

he let him not lord over them, saying, - **It is not I who is talking**, for every time one is haughty, he takes away a little bit of his reward.

ויענה **אמן** על כל ברכה, כי גדול העונה **אמן** יותר מן המברך, ופותחים לו שערי גן עדן.
Now let him respond **amen** to each and every blessing. For the one who responds **amen** is greater than the one who says the blessing and the gates of paradise open for him.

ויהא שמה רבא מברך, יענה בכל כוחו בפיו ובכל כוונתו.
At **may His great name be blessed**... let him respond with all his ability with his mouth and with all his concentration.

ולא יצא מבית הכנסת בשעת קריאת התורה, אם לא בין גברא לגברא.
And he should not leave the synagogue during the reading of the Torah if not between a man and his fellow.

לעולם, בין בשעת תפלה ובין בשעת ברכת המזון, כל שעה שאדם עסוק לדבר לשכינה, לא יגע בבשרו.
As long as a man is busy speaking of the **Shekhinah** [The presence of God] between the time of prayer and the time of the grace after meals, he shall not be plagued.

כי אם בידיים עד הפרק העליון, ובצווארו עד חלוקו, אבל לא ברגליו, ולא בכל שאר בשרו ובמנעליו. ואם נגע - ייטול ידיו או ישפשפן בעפר או בקיסם.

Sefer HaYirah / ספר הירֹאה

Except in his hands up to the forearm, or in his neck as far as the shirt, but not in his legs, and not in all the rest of his flesh or his feet. But if he is plagued let him wash his hands or rub them with dust or with pebbles or with wood chips.

ואם יצטרך לחכך, יחכך מעל לחלוקו. ואל יגע לא בכינה, ולא בשער בית השחי ובית הערווה. ואם נגע, ייטול ידיו או ישפשפן בעפר או בצרור או בקיסם.

But if he needs to scratch, let him scratch over his undershirt; and he must not touch neither a cavity nor the hair of the arm pit nor the area of the genitals. But if he does touch them, he should wash his hands or rub them with dust, pebbles, or wood chips.

ובשעת תפלה, טפח מגולה אפילו באשתו, ערווה, ואסור לקרות שמע ולהתפלל ולהסתכל בה.

Now if at the time of prayer, a hands breadth is exposed even to his wife of genital area, then it is forbidden to recite - **Shema** or to pray or look upon it.

Sefer HaYirah   ספר הירֵאה

אחרי בית הכנסת After the synagogue

ויצא מבית הכנסת בנחת ובדרך כריעה, ויאמר - ה'[23] נחני בצדקתך למען שוררי הישר לפני דרכך. וילך.

Then he goes out from the synagogue, humbly and in a bowing manner, he says - O LORD, lead me along Your righteous path because of my watchful foes make Your way straight before me. then he goes.

ובלכתו בדרך, אל ישוח יותר מדי, ואל ישפיל סודרו על עיניו, פן יחשב ללעג.

But when he goes on his way, he should not bend too much. And he should not lower his scarf over his eyes lest he be thought a mockery.

ואל ילך בקומה זקופה. כי ההולך בקומה זקופה, דומה כמסלק המורא מעליו. אלא ילך במידה בינונית, לא זקוף ולא כפוף יותר מדי, אלא שלא יראה הבא כנגדו בפניו.

Nor should he walk with proud carriage for one who walks at his full stature is like one who suspends the fear **of heaven** from upon him? But rather he should walk in an average manner, not erect but not too bent. Rather so that he should not look one who comes in front of him in the face.

וישפיל עיניו, שלא יראה את חברו כנגדו כמלוא עיניו.

Let him lower his eyes so that he should not

---

[23] תהלים ה ט

Sefer HaYirah   ספר הירא͏ה

look his fellow right in the eye.

ואם פגע דבר ערווה, כגון אישה, בין יהודית בין ארמית, בין נשואה בין פנויה, בין גדולה בין קטנה, יעצום עיניו או יסובב לצד אחר, כדי שלא יראנה. וכן אמר החכם, אין לך דבר חוצץ בפני התאווה כעצימת העין.

And if he should come in contact with a thing of nakedness such as a woman, whether Jewish or gentile, whether married or single, whether big or small, he should close his eyes or turn his face aside so that he shall not see her. And so said the sage. You have no such barrier faced with of sexual desire as the closing of the eye.

וכן אם פגע בחזיר וחזירה, או כל בהמה נזקקים זו לזו, אל יסתכל בהם.

And the same if he should come in contact with and boar and a sow, or any animal in intercourse with each other he must not look upon them.

ויהיה מקדים בשלום כל אדם, אפילו אינו ישראל, כדי שיהיה אהוב ונחמד לבריות.

And he should be the first to greet every man, even a gentile so that he should be beloved and precious to God's creatures.

אך לא בשלום אישה. ויבוא לביתו בשלום.

But he should not greet a woman, so that he may return to his home and family in peace.

ויסיר תפילין ויתנם בכיס, של יד על של ראש.

Sefer HaYirah / ספר היראה

Then he should take off his tefillin, and put them in the bag, the hand piece on top of the head piece.

ויסיר של ראש תחלה ואחר כך של יד. ויסיר מכנסיו וילבש אחרים.

He should take off the head-piece first, and the hand-piece second, then he should take off his pants and put on other ones.

וטוב שילמד מיד, משום דכתיב - ילכו[24] מחיל אל חיל, ומיד טרם ילך לעסקיו.

And it would be good for him to learn Torah immediately, since it is written - they go from strength to strength. immediately, before he goes out to his business.

ואם הוא אדם חלוש ורגיל בפת שחרית, יאכל מיד.

But if he be a weak man and accustomed to breakfast, let him eat immediately.

ויטול ידיו תחלה בהרבה מים, ולכל הפחות ייטול מים רביעית הלוג.

But he should wash his hands first with a lot of water. At the very least he should wash with a quarter log [A Talmudic unit of liquid measurement roughly equal to 6 eggs, as equal to large glass] of water.

וייתן שלוש פעמים מים על ידיו.

Let him pour water over his hands three times.

---

[24] תהילים פד ח

Sefer HaYirah ספר היראה

וישפשפן היטב. ושלא יהא דבר חוצץ, כי כל החוצץ בטבילה, חוצץ בנטילת ידים.
And let him rub them well, so that there should be no barrier, for any barrier to immersion in a mikveh, is a barrier to ritual handwashing.

ויגביהן בנטילה, שלא יחזרו מים הראשונים ויטמאו את הידיים.
He should raise them in the washing so that the first waters do not drip down, and ritually impurify his hands.

וינגבן היטב.
Then let him dry them very well.

ויברך על הלחם המוציא. וייתן ריווח בין תיבה לתיבה.
Now he blesses **Hamotzi** over the bread, but he must leave an interval between each and every letter.

וכל מה שייהנה בו מן העולם הזה, בין בפירות, בין בריח, בין באכילה, בין בכל דבר שייהנה, אסור ליהנות בלא ברכה. ויברך בכל דבר לפניו ולאחריו הברכה האמורה בה על פי רבותינו עליהם השלום.
And everything from this world that he may enjoy, whether in fruits or in scent or in eating or any other thing that he may enjoy, it is forbidden to enjoy without a blessing. And let him bless every thing with the blessing that was said by our Rabbis before it and after it, may peace be upon them.

Sefer HaYirah ספר הירא֫ה

ואם אינו בקי, ילך אצל בקי ללמוד, ואל ישים עצמו כבהמה. ואם לא מצא בקי, ילך ויניח הנאתו, ולא ייהנה מן הדבר עד שידע לברך עליו את בוראו כדת וכמשפט.

Now, if he has no expert in blessings let him go to an expert to learn and not make himself like a dumb animal. But if he does not find an expert he goes and leaves his enjoyment of it. And he shall not enjoy any thing until he knows how to bless its Creator over it according to the law.

וכשיברך, יכוון את לבו לברך את הבורא, ולא כדבר הרגיל בפי אדם לצאת שלא בכוונה. וכן לברכת המצות וכל מעשה האדם יעשה, יעשה דברים לשם פעלם ולא מצות אנשים מלומדה ומנהג אבות.

Now when he blesses let him direct his heart to bless the Creator and not as a thing that is a habit in the mouth of a man to come out without proper intention. And so too with the blessing over a mitzvah. And any deed that a person may do, let him do things for the sake of doing them and not as a commandment trained by people and an ancestral custom.

ומאוד יהיה צנוע באכילתו.

He should have excellent manners when he eats.

ואחר גמר סעודתו יברך ברכת המזון.

And after he finishes his meal, he should recite the blessing of the food.

Sefer HaYirah   ספר היראה

ואחר כך ישתה מים או יין להשלים מאה ברכות ביום.
Afterwards, let him drink water or wine to complete one hundred blessings in a day.

והכל לשם שמים.
And all of these blessings for the sake of heaven.

Sefer HaYirah ספר היראה

עסקים Business

וטרם ילך לעסקיו, ילמד פסוק או הלכה, כדי לקיים מצוות והגית[25] בו יומם ולילה.

Before he goes to his work, let him learn one verse of Torah or one law to fulfill the mitzvah of - you shall meditate on it day and night.

ואותה שעה ילמד בהגיון הלב, ולהיות אוזניו ועיניו פקוחות אל אשר מוציא בשפתיו.

At the same time let him learn with musing of the heart. And let his ears and his eyes be open to what his lips bring forth.

ואל יפסיק משנתו לדברים בטלים, כי אף לומר - מה[26] נאה אילן זה, מה נאה ניר זה, אשר יש בו דבר שבח, שמברכים עליהם ברוך שככה לו בעולמו, הרי זה מתחייב בנפשו. קל וחמר לשיחת חולין, אשר כל דברי עבירה תלויים בה.

Let him not break off from his study for idle things. For even saying - **How beautiful is this tree**. Or - **How beautiful is that field**. in which there is an excellent thing such that one would recite, Blessed is the One who has such in His world, over it, why, this one is liable for the death penalty. How much the more so for profane chatter, upon which all words of sin hang.

והשחת[27] בהם עובר בלאו ועשה. **עשה** - ודברת[28] בם. ולא

---

[25] יהושע א ח
[26] משנה אבות ג ד
[27] יומא יט ב
[28] דברים ו ז

ספר היראה — Sefer HaYirah

בדברים אחרים, ולאו הבא מכלל עשה, עשה. **ולאו** - כל[29] הדברים יגעים לא יוכל איש לדבר.

And one who chatters on them transgresses both a negative and a positive commandment. The positive commandment to - **Speak upon them**. not of other things. And the negative commandment comes from the positive commandment - what it says to do, do and what it says not to do, do not do. And the negative - **All such things are wearisome; no man can ever state them**.

וכל שכן להפסיק מדברי תורה שהוא חייב לעסוק בהם. ועל המפסיקים נאמר - הקוטפים[30] מלוח עלי שיח ושרש רתמים לחמם. ואמרו רבותינו - כל[31] הפוסק מדברי תורה ועוסק בדברי שיחה, מאכילין אותו גחלי רתמים בגיהנם.

Moreover, everyone who does break off from words of Torah are obligated to engage in them. And about those who break off from Torah it is said - **They cut up mallows by the bushes, and roots of broom for warmth**. And our sages of blessed memory said - **All those who break off from words of Torah to engage in idle chatter, they feed them fiery coals in Geihinnom** [Tree of Retama raetam].

אחרי כן ילך לעסקיו, כי יפה דרך ארץ, ולא יוכל אדם לעבוד את הבורא אם לא יטרח לבקש מזונותיו. וכן אמר

---

[29] קהלת א ח
[30] איוב ל ד
[31] חגיגה יב ב

Sefer HaYirah   ספר היראה

דוד - אשרי[32] כל ירא ה' ההלך בדרכיו. יגיע[33] כפיך כי תאכל אשריך וטוב לך.

After learning Torah, he should go to his business, for it is good to earn a living no one can serve the Creator if he is busy begging for his meals. And thus said King David - **Happy is everyone who fears the LORD who walks in his ways. For you shall eat the labor of your hands.**

ויהיו עסקיו באמונה.

Now his business shall be conducted faithfully.

וירחק מדבר שקר.

And he should keep away from lying words.

ומחברת אנשים רעים.

Or from bad company.

וממושב לצים.

Or an assembly of scoffers.

ואם יצטרך לשבת עמהם פן ילעיגו ויתלוצצו עליו ויראה כעושה עצמו חשוב, אל ייכנס לתוך דבריהם ואל ישיב להם כי אם בקוצר רוח, ויקום מיד שיוכל.

But if he must sit with them - In case they mock and make light of him and he should appear as one who puffs himself up let him not interrupt their words or reply to them except with shortness of breath and let him get up as

---

[32] תהילים קכח א
[33] תהילים קכח ב

Sefer HaYirah ספר היראה

immediately as he is able.

ויזהר בלי להונות את חברו לא בדברים, וקל וחומר בממון.
Let him take care not to treat his fellow overbearingly neither with words, all the more so with money.

ואף עסקו עם הנוכרי יהיה באמונה, פן יתחלל שם שמים ותורת ישראל תתבזה על ידו.
Even his business with the **Gentile** should be with faith, lest he desecrate the name of Heaven and the Torah of Israel be despised by his hand.

ואם ישמע מוציאי דיבה על איש, אל יאמין להם, כי שמא הם שונאיו, אלא יעשה עצמו כמאמין, ואל יאמין.
But if he should hear evil reports about a man, he should not believe them, for it may be that they are of his enemies, rather act like he believes without actually believing.

ואם יקללהו אדם ויחרפהו, אל ישיב לו מאומה, ויהיה נעלב ולא עולב.
Now, if a person should curse him or revile him, he should not reply anything at all, but let him submit to humiliation and not humiliate.

ואל יצא לריב מהר.
Neither let him be quick to go out to quarrel.

ואל יבוא אצל בני אדם, שהם מתלחשים יחד.
He should not stay with people whispering together.

Sefer HaYirah

ואל יוציא דיבה על שום אדם ואפילו הוא שונאו.
Nor should he give evil reports about anyone, even his enemy.

ואל ישנא בלבבו כי אם את אשר המקום שנא.
And let him not hate in his heart, except what the Omnipresent One hates.

וכל ענינו ועסקו יהא לשם שמים.
Every business dealing of his should be for the sake of Heaven.

ובשובו מעסקיו, אל ישב בטל, כי מה לאדם להיות יושב בטל, הלא הבטלה מביאה לידי שעמום ולידי הרהורים רעים, אף כי תלמוד תורה אין לו שעור.
When he returns from his business, he should not sit idly, for what does it do for a man to be sitting idly, does not laziness bring him into the hands of stupefaction and impure fancies, whereas there is no end to the reward of learning Torah.

Sefer HaYirah   ספר היראה

בבית ואורחים At home and guests

ואם יבאו אורחים לביתו, יכניסם לביתו בסבר פנים יפות.
If guests should come to his house, he should welcome them with a cheerful countenance.

ומיד בבואם ישים לפניהם לחם לאכול, כי פעמים בא העני ולא אכל והוא בוש לשאול.
And as soon as they come, he should set bread before them to eat for sometimes a poor person may come who has not eaten but is ashamed to ask.

וייתן להם לחמו ומימיו ואת אשר יאכל, בפנים מאירות. ואף אם יהיה בלבבו עצב ודאגה, ישיחנה מליבו בפניהם.
Now let him give them his bread and his water and what he might eat to brighten their faces. But even if there should be sorrow and worry in his heart let him warm his heart in front of them.

וינחמם בדבריו ויהי להם למשיב נפש.
And put them at rest with his words, and be for them a restorer of the soul.

ואפילו אם יהיו לו אלף עבדים, יטרח הוא בעצמו, ויעמוד עליהם, כי מי לנו גדול מאברהם ששימש למלאכים, והיו לו כמה עבדים ושפחות, שנאמר, ואת[34] כל ילידי ביתו. ואף[35] על פי שנראו כערביים. כדברי רבותינו זיכרונם לברכה, ובכל מה שעשה על ידי עצמו, שילם לו הקדוש

---

[34] בראשית יז כג
[35] בבא מציעא פו ב

Sefer HaYirah   ספר הַיִראָה

ברוך הוא לישראל בכבודו ובעצמו.

And even if he may have a thousand servants, he should serve them himself. Who do we have as great as Abraham who served the messengers of the Lord, but had many manservants and maidservants, as it is said - And all his homeborn slaves, and all those he had bought? And despite that they appeared like Arabs according to our Rabbis of blessed memory. And with everything that Abraham did by himself, the Holy One Blessed Be He repaid on his behalf to Israel in His dignity and Himself.

ואל יספר לפניהם, כך וכך אירע לי, מקצת תלאותיו, כי דברים אלו שוברים את רוחם, כמדומה להם כי בשבילם אמר כן, וכמעט אין לו שכר בעמלו.

He should not recount before them, such and such happened to me, from some of his troubles, for these words shatter their spirits, appearing to them that for their sake he says so and that he hardly has any money in his purse.

ויכבדם כאדונים לו. וכן מצינו באברהם - שקראם[36] **אדונים**. וגדול[37] הכנסתם יותר מקבלת פני השכינה.

But let him honor them as his lords. And so, we find with Abraham, who called them **My Lords**. And greater was welcoming them than receiving the face of the **Shekhinah** [The presence of God].

---

[36] בראשית יח ג

[37] שבת קכז א

Sefer HaYirah

ובשעת האוכל יראה את עצמו כמצטער שאינו יכול להיטיב להם יותר. וכן הוא אומר - ותפק[38] לרעב נפשך. ויאמר לו, תצא נפשי שאין לי מה לתן לך.

And at meal time, he should show himself as one who grieves that he is not able to prepare more for them, and so it says - If you draw out your soul to the hungry. Therefore, say to him. I am dying that I have no more to give you.

ואם ילינו אצלו, ישכיבם במיטב מטותיו, כי גדולה מנוחת העיף בהיותו שוכב בטוב, ויותר עושה לו נחת רוח המשכיבו היטב יותר מן המאכילו ומשקהו, וגלגל הוא החוזר בעולם.

So, if they should stay with him, he should lay them down in the best of his beds, for it is greater to rest the weary than to be well rested. And giving his guest rest makes more rest for him than to feed him or slake his thirst. And it comes back to him in the next world.

ובצאתם ילוום וייתן להם פת צדה לדרך.

And when they leave, he should accompany them.

כי[39] על פת לחם יפשע גבר. כי[40] על אשר לא נתן יהונתן לדוד פת לחם בהיפרדו מאתו. נתגלגל הדבר ונהרגו כהני נוב, שמונים וחמשה איש נושאי אפוד בד. והענק[41] תעניק להם מסת נדבת ידך.

He should give them a bit of provision for the

---

[38] ישעיה נח י
[39] משלי כח כא
[40] סנהדרין קד א
[41] דברים טז י

Sefer HaYirah   ספר היראה

road, for a man will transgress for a piece of bread. For since Jonathan did not give David a piece of bread when he parted from him the thing caused the priests [city] of **Nov** to be killed, eighty-five men who wore the linen Ephod. And you shall surely press gifts upon them according to the donation of your hand.

Sefer HaYirah ספר היראה

With people עם אנשים

ואם באה מצווה לידך, תמהר בה ואל תתרשל בה, כי[42] זהירות מביאה לידי זריזות, נקיות, פרישות, טהרה, קדושה, יראת חטא, חסידות, וענוה.

If you have the opportunity to do a **Mitzvah** make haste to do it and do not be relaxed about it. For caution brings one into zeal, cleanliness, separation, purity, holiness, fear of sin, piety, and humility.

ויהא זהיר בכבוד חכמים. בא חכם אצלך, תקבל פניו בכבוד וכבדהו.

Be cautious with the honor of the sages. If a sage should come to your home, welcome him with honor and honor him.

יש חתן בעיר, לך ועסוק בו ושמחהו, כי המשמחו זוכה לראות בשמחת ירושלים.

If there is a groom in the city, go outfit him and rejoice with him, for one who rejoices with him merits seeing the redemption of Jerusalem.

יש מת בעיר, טרח בו ויספדהו, אך במידה בינונית, כי אין כבודו לומר מה שלא היה בו, ושתיקה יפה. אך המידות אשר ידעת אשר היו בו טובות, תספר, ותלוהו.

If there is a death in the city, attend to the dead and mourn him. Even in a middling aspect for it does not honor him to tell beyond what he had, and silence is beautiful. Only those good characteristics which you know that he had you

---

[42] עבודה זרה כ ב

Sefer HaYirah   ספר הירָאה

shall tell and you shall escort him.

אם יש ברית מילה בעיר, טרח ועסוק והיה כמסיע במצווה, כי⁴³ גדול שכר מסיע כעושה המצווה.
If there is a **BRIT** [circumcision] to be done, in the city, attend to him and be as one who assists in the mitzvah, for the reward of the one who assists is as great as of the one who does the mitzvah.

ואם⁴⁴ חבריך בצרה, היה צר בצרתם.
If your fellows are in distress be distressed in their distress.

ואל תשמח בעת כישלונם, והיה שמח בטובתם.
Do not rejoice in their downfall, but be happy at their good fortune.

שמעת צרת ישראל הרחוקים, האנח והתפלל עליהם, וכל שכן על הקרובים.
Moreover, if you have heard of the distress of Jews far away, cry and pray for them, and just as much for those near by.

ברך את הצור על כל הבא, על הטוב ועל הרע. תשמח בייסורים ותחשוב הכל לטובה, בכל מידה ומידה שהוא מודד לך, וזהו שכתוב - ובכל⁴⁵ מאודך. ואל תבעט בייסורים, ותחשוב הכל לטובה. ואמור - כל⁴⁶ דעביד רחמנא לטב עביד.

---
⁴³ מכות ה ב
⁴⁴ על פי - ברכות יב ב
⁴⁵ דברים ו ה
⁴⁶ ברכות ס ב

Sefer HaYirah ספר היראה

Bless the Rock of Israel over everything that comes, over the good and over the bad, rejoice in suffering and consider everything for good, with each and every measure that He measures out for you. And this is - "And with all your might. And do not be contumacious in suffering, but consider it all for the good, and say - Whatever the Merciful One does is for good.

והתרחק מן הנדרים, כי בעוון הנדרים בנים מתים, ואשתו[47] של אדם מתה.

Keep away from vows, for on account of broken vows children die and a man's wife dies.

ומן השבועות.

And from oaths.

ומן הכעס. כי כל הכועס, מבלבל דעתו ורוחו ולא יתיצב באהבת הבורא. וכן אמרו רבותינו - לא[48] תרתח ולא תחטא. ובכמה מקומות דבר שלמה בחכמתו - והסר[49] כעס מלבך. כי[50] כעס בחיק כסילים ינוח. הרגזן[51] לא עלה בידו אלא רגזנותו. וגם משה רבנו שהיה אב לחכמים ולנביאים, כל מקום שבא לכלל כעס, בא לכלל טעות.

And from anger, for anyone that becomes angry mixes up his reason with his spirit, and will not place himself in the love of the Creator. And so, our Rabbis said - Do not get hot and

---

[47] שבת לב ב
[48] ברכות כט ב
[49] קהלת יא י
[50] קהלת ז ט
[51] קידושין מ ב

Sefer HaYirah ספר היראה

you will not sin. And in several places King Solomon said in his wisdom. Remove anger from your heart. For anger rests in the bosom of fools. Nothing will come to the hand of a quarrelsome person but his irritability. And even with Moses our teacher, who was the greatest of the sages and the prophets, whenever he was under the influence of anger he came under the influence of mistaken judgment.

בא לכלל טעות. ואפילו אם עשה לך אדם שלא כהוגן, אל תקפיד, ולמוד מהלל ענותן זכרונו לברכה.
Even if someone treats you inappropriately, do not lose your temper. But learn from Hillel the modest one, of blessed memory.

ואף להטיל אימה בתוך ביתו, מצווה להראות עצמו כעסן ודעתו מיושבת ורוחו נחה, ואל יטיל אימה יתרה.
The same goes for fear inside his home - It is a Mitzvah to show himself like one who can get angry, but whose mind is settled. But he should not develop additional fear, but only a moderate amount.

ואל ישבר יקרע כליו בחמתו, אף לא ישחית כל מאומה.
He should not smash dishes in his anger. He should not destroy anything at all.

ויאכוף את יצרו מכל אשר יתאווה, אף משיחה בטלה. כי מה יתרון בדברים שלא לצורך, אין זה כי אם הרבות פשע.
Let him bend his inclination from anything

Sefer HaYirah   ספר היראה

which he may enjoy, even from idle chatter, for what gain is there in needless words? This is nothing but increasing liability for negligence.

והוי רצוי לאחיך ולחבריך.
Be beloved to your brothers, and to your fellows.

ואל תשכב בלילה וקטטה לך עם אדם, אך לך ותרצה אותו עד שיתפייס. ואף אם חטא לך, בקש ממנו פיוס. ואל תאמר, הן חטא לי, ועליו לבוא לפייסני, כוף את יצרך ולך אליו, למען לא יגבה לבבך ותהיה מתועב לפני הבורא, שנאמר - תועבת[52] ה' כל גבה לב.

You shall not even lie down at night if you have a quarrel with a person. But go and appease him until you both reconcile. But even if he has sinned against you, seek reconciliation from him. Do not say - See he has sinned against me, it is up to him to reconcile with me, bend your inclination and go to him, so that your heart shall not grow proud and you shall be abominable in the eyes of the Creator. As it is said - "Every proud heart is an abomination to the LORD,

ומאוד הזהר שלא לשקר, אפילו בדברי הבאי, כי חילול השם יש בדבר. ואף לא להשתכר בשקר, כי יצא שכרו בהפסדו, כי הוא - מארבע[53] כיתות שאינן מקבלות פני השכינה, כת משקרים, כת חנפים, כת לצים, וכת מספרי לשון הרע.

---

[52] משלי טז ה
[53] סוטה מב א

Sefer HaYirah / ספר היראה

Be especially careful not to lie, even in a word of a rhetorical phrase, for there is desecration of the Divine Name in speech. And also, not to be rewarded in a lie, for the gain will be offset by the loss, since the four classes of those who will not receive the face of the **Shekhinah** [The presence of God] - the class of liars, the class of hypocrites, the class of scoffers and the class of slanderers.

וכן[54] עונשו של בדאי, שאפילו אומר אמת, אין שומעים לו.
And such is the punishment of the liar, that even if he speaks the truth, no one believes him.

וכל[55] המחליף בדבורו, כאלו עובד עבודה זרה, דכתיב הכא - והייתי[56] בעיניו כמתעתע. וכתיב התם - הבל[57] המה מעשה תעתועים.
And anyone who repeats his speech is as if he were an idol worshipper. As is written in this case - I shall seem to him a deceiver. Regarding anyone who changes his words is written - They are vanity, the work of delusion.

והזהר מן הליצנות, כי היא שניה לעברות, והיא מעבירה את המורא ומרגילה את האדם לעבור. וכל[58] המתלוצץ נופל בגיהנם.
Now take care to avoid scoffing, for it is the second of the transgressions. For it transgresses

---

[54] סנהדרין פט ב
[55] סנהדרין צב א
[56] בראשית כז יב
[57] ירמיהו י טו
[58] עבודה זרה יח ב

Sefer HaYirah ספר היראה

against the fear of Heaven. And it accustoms a person to transgress. Every one who speaks frivolously falls into the Valley of Death.

ושלא להחניף, כי - לא[59] לפניו חנף יבוא.
And that he not be hypocritical - For a hypocrite shall not come before Him.

ושלא לספר לשון הרע, כי[60] לכל יש רפואה חוץ מלשון הרע.
And that he not tells slander, for everything has a cure but slander.

ושלא לקבלו, שנאמר - לא[61] תשא שמע שוא.
And that he not listens to it, as is said - You must not carry false rumors.

והתרחק מן הכבוד, וכבד כל אדם.
And one should keep away from honor, but honor every person.

ותעביר על מידותיך.
You shall turn away from your own characteristics.

והוי[62] דן את כל אדם לכף זכות, למען יעבירו מן השמים על פשעיך וידונו אותך לכף זכות.
Judge everyone in the scale of merit, for the

---

[59] איוב יג טז
[60] פרקי דרבי אליעזר נד
[61] שמות כג א
[62] שבת קכז ב

Sefer HaYirah

sake that in Heaven they shall overlook your sins and judge you in the scale of merit.

Sefer HaYirah — ספר היראה

כבוד אב ואם וחכם Honor father and mother and sage

ואם אתה אצל בני אדם שחייב אתה בכבודם, כגון אביך ואימך, כבדם ותירא מהם.

If you are with people that you are obligated to honor, such as your father and your mother honor them and be **fearful** of them.

ולא תשב במקומם.

And you shall not sit in their place.

ולא תסתור את דבריהם, אם אמרו דבר אפילו ידעת כי איננו כן, אל תאמר לא כן היה.

And you shall not contradict their words, if they say something, even if you know that it is not so. Do not say - **It was not so**.

ואם יש להם דבר עם אדם, אל תכריע ביניהם.

And if they have a word with a person, do not compromise between them.

ואל תכנס לתוך דבריהם, כי אף תוך דברי חברו אם נכנס בהם, נקרא גולם.

Do not interrupt them, for even one who interrupts his fellow is called a fool.

כללו של דבר, כל מה שיוכל לתלות הכבוד בהם, יתלה, ולא בו.

The rule of the matter - everything that might be attached to their honor should be attached and not to his.

Sefer HaYirah   ספר הירא͏ה

ומאוד יש להיזהר בכבודם, כי הוקש כבודם לכבוד המקום, והמכבדם כאלו כיבד את המקום. והמצערם כאלו צער עצמו.

One must be very careful with their honor, for their honor is compared to the honor of the One Who Is Everywhere, and one who honors them is as if he honors the One Who Is Everywhere, but one who causes them pain is as if he pains himself.

וחייב להאכילם ולהשקותם ולהלבישם ולהכניסם ולהוציאם.

Further, he is obligated to feed them, give them drink, dress them, bring them in and take them out.

ואם אין לו, ייסוב על הפתחים וייתן להם.

But if he does not have anything for them, let him go knock on the doorways of people's homes and beg and give the alms to them.

ומה שיעשה להם, דרך כבוד יעשה, כי[63] יש מאכיל אביו פסיוני, וטורדן מן העולם. ומטחינו ברחיים, ומביאו לחיי העולם הבא.

And whatever he may do for them, let it be by way of honoring them. For one person may feed his father pheasant and drive him out of the world but someone else may make his father grind in the mill and bring him into everlasting life in the world to come.

---

[63] קידושין לא א

Sefer HaYirah ספר היראה

היה אביו עובר על דברי תורה, אל יאמר לו, אבא, עברת על דברי תורה, אלא אומר לו, מקרא כתוב בתורה כך הוא. והוא יבין מעצמו, ואל תבישו.

If his father transgressed the words of the Torah, he must not say to him - Father, you have transgressed the words of the Torah, but rather he says to him, the verse is written in the Torah like so. And he shall understand on his own and he shall not be disgraced.

ולא ידבר על מעשיהם בשום עניין, אפילו[64] זרק ארנקו לים או לאור בפניו, לא יכלימנו.

And he should not speak of their deeds in any matter, even if he throws his money bag into the sea or into the fire in front of him, do not rebuke him.

ואם שמע אדם מדבר עליהם שלא כהוגן, יקהה שניו ויאמר לו, שקר אתה דובר. אך אין להכות את חברו על כך, ואף שתיקה יפה במקום שאין כבודם, כמו שהוא יודע, שאם ימחה אז יוסיף האחר לומר עליהם דברי גנאי אחרים.

But if he hears a person speaking about them improperly, blunt his teeth and say to him, you are telling a lie. But there is no striking his fellow over such. But even silence is appropriate in a place where the parents are not dishonored. As in the case where he knows if he shall protest, then the other shall add; the dignity of the parents would not be served by a reply.

---

[64] קידושין לא ב

Sefer HaYirah

ורצונם הוא כבודם.
And their will is their honor.

ואם⁶⁵ שמחלו על כבודם, כבודם מחול.
And they that wipe out their honor, their honor is wiped out.

והוי ירא מן החכמים, כמו⁶⁶ שדרש רבי עקיבה - את⁶⁷ ה' אלוהי"ך תירא. לרבות תלמידי חכמים.
And be in awe of the sages, as Rabbi Akiva expounded, on the verse - You shall fear the lord your God, including the disciples of the sages.

והדבק⁶⁸ בהם ובדרכיהם הטובים.
Cleave unto them and their ways of the good.

ועמוד מפניהם, ואף⁶⁹ מפני הזקנים שאינם חכמים. ובטל⁷⁰ רצונך מפני רצונם.
And stand up before them, even before elders that are not sages and nullify your will before their will.

וכבד את אחיך הגדול, ואחי אביך, ואחי אימך, ובעל אימך, ואשת אביך, כי בכולם דרשו חכמים⁷¹ מן המקרא שכתוב - כבד⁷² את אביך ואת אימך.

---

⁶⁵ קידושין לב א
⁶⁶ פסחים כב ב
⁶⁷ דברים ו יג
⁶⁸ פסחים מט א
⁶⁹ ויקרא יט לב
⁷⁰ פרקי אבות ב ד
⁷¹ כתובות קג א
⁷² שמות כ יא

Sefer HaYirah   ספר היראה

And honor your elder brother, And the brother of your father, And the brother of your mother. And the husband of your mother. And the wife of your father. For on all of them the sages of blessed memory, expounded from the verse - Honor your father and your mother,

אל תרדוף אחר ישיבת עמי הארץ ולצים, כי מהם לא תלמד חכמה, כי אם דברים ריקים ולצון.
Do not seek out a gathering of ignoramuses or scoffers, because from them you shall not learn wisdom, but only empty words and scoffing.

אך רדוף אחר החכמים, כי[73] מהם תלמד חכמה.
But seek out the sages because from them you shall learn wisdom.

ואל[74] תהי בז לדברי אחיך, ואל תלעג לשום אדם.
And do not be contemptuous of the words of your brother, and do not mock any person.

אל[75] תמנע טוב מבעליו. אם שאלך אדם על טובה שבעולם, או דבר מצווה, אל תמנענו מלעשותה, אך אם אין דעתך על הדבר, אמור לו - עשה כחכמתך.
Do not withhold good from one who deserves it If a person asks you for a favor or for a mitzvah, do not refuse to do it. But if you have no knowledge about the matter, say to him - Do according to your wisdom.

---

[73] פרקי אבות ו ט
[74] פרקי אבות ד ג
[75] משלי ג כז

Sefer HaYirah   ספר היראה

עזרה לזולת Helping Others

והיה רגיל בצדקה כפי כוחך, ולכל הפחות שעבד עצמך לבורא לתת כופר נפשך חוק קבוע בכל שבוע פרוטה או מחצה, כי - אפילו[76] עני המתפרנס מן הצדקה יש לו לעשות צדקה.

Be accustomed to giving as much **Tzedakah** [Charity] as you can at the very least discipline yourself to ransom your soul. A fixed law. every week a **Pruta** [A small coin of money] or a half. Rhymed mnemonic in original. For even a poor person who is supported from tzedakah must give Tzedakah.

וכשתיתן לעני, תן לו **בסתר**, כי - מתן[77] בסתר יכפה אף.

When you give to the poor, give in **secret**, for - A gift in secret averts anger.

ועניך קודמין.

And your poor people take precedence.

ואל[78] תקפוץ ידך. מהלוות לעני בשעת דחקו, כי גדול המלווה יותר מן העושה צדקה, וצדקתו[79] עומדת לעד. כי איננו חסר בדבר, ויחשוב כי לכמה נכרים הוא מלווה בלא ריבית.

And do not close your hand from lending to the poor at their most urgent time. For greater is the one who lends than the one who gives **Tzedakah** [Charity], and his righteousness

---

[76] גיטין ז ב
[77] משלי כא יד
[78] דברים טו ז
[79] תהלים קיב ג

Sefer HaYirah   ספר היראה

endures forever. For he does not lose the principal, and he should consider for how many gentiles he lends without interest.

ואם יקשה בעיניו להלוותו בלא משכון, ילונו במשכון, ויקבע לו זמן להלוואתו. ובתוך ימי ההלוואה לא יקראהו לעשות מלאכתו או כל דבר אם לא ייתן לו שכרו מושלם, שנראה[80] כריבית.

But if it should be difficult in his eyes to lend without collateral, let him lend with collateral and set for him a time to pay it back. But during the term of the loan, he is not to call upon him to do his labor or any thing if he will not pay him his complete salary, since it would be seen as interest.

ובמעשרות, אל תרפה ידיך מלינתה כראוי. כיצד? מכל דבר שמשתכר, הן ללמד, הן לכתוב, הן לעשות מלאכה, או אף אם מצא מציאה, או נתנו לו במתנה, או כל עניין שיהיה, הן כסף הן שווה זהב, מן הכל יפריש מעשר, כי דבר זה אין לו ערך, כי את אשר אסר הבורא בכל דבר לנסותו, התיר במעשר[81].

And in tithes, do not let your hand be lax from removing what is appropriate. How? From everything that he profits, whether to teach, whether to write, whether to do labor, or even if he should find a finding, or if they gave it to him as a gift, or anything that may come to be whether money, or money's value, from everything let him set aside the tithe, for this

---

[80] בבא מציעא סד ב
[81] תענית ט א

Sefer HaYirah / ספר היראה

thing has no value, since everything which the Creator forbids to try him in any case, He permits in tithing.

אל תגנוב דעת הבריות ואפילו דעתו של גוי, ואל תסרב בחברך יותר מדי. ואל תאמר לו, דבר זה עשיתי בשבילך, ולא עשית בשבילו. אך אם יטעה וידמה כי בשבילו עשית, אין צריך לומר לו, לא עשיתי בעבורך, כי הוא מטעה את עצמו, ואין זה גנבת-דעת.

Do not deceive God's creations, even gentiles. Do not hustle your fellow too much. And do not say to him -I have done this thing for you, if you did not do it for him. But if he should err and it should seem that for him you have done it, there is no need to tell him - I did not do it for your sake, for he has erred on his own and this is not deception.

כללו של דבר, כל צד גנבת דעת, אסורה.

The rule of the matter is - all forms of deception are forbidden.

Sefer HaYirah ספר היראה

דבור נקי Clean speech

אל[82] תזכיר שם שמים לבטלה, כי המזכיר שם שמים לבטלה, ראוי לנדותו. אף שלא לצורך במקום מטונף.
Do not mention the name of Heaven in vain, for anyone who takes the name of Heaven in vain should be excommunicated. And not even of necessity should one mention the Divine God Name in a filthy place.

ולא תשבע כלל, ואף לא בכינויים, ואף לא במידותיו ובמעשיו, כגון שמשיו ומשרתיו מלאכי מעלה.
Do not mention the name of Heaven in vain, for anyone who takes the name of Heaven in vain should be excommunicated. And not even of necessity should one mention the Divine God Name in a filthy place.

וכן לא ישבע בתורה ולא באמת, כי השם נקרא אמת, וה'[83] אלהי"ם אמת.
And thus, he should not swear on the Torah nor on truth, for God is called Truth - But the lord is a true God.

ולא יקלל חברו בשם, אף לא עצמו כה יעזרני השם[84].
And he should not curse his fellow by the Name, nor even himself by saying - so help me God.

---

[82] נדרים ז ב
[83] ירמיה י י
[84] עיין שבועות לה א

ספר היראה   Sefer HaYirah

ואל יישמע שום שם טומאה על שפתיך, כמו שמות הקדשים יעקרו ויהרסו. וכשתזכירם לצורך בפני הגויים, אמור[85] בשפה רפה ובכובד ראש.

And let no impure name be heard upon your lips like the names of the Sodomites, may they be uprooted and destroyed! But when you must mention them in front of the gentiles speak in an undertone and with solemnity.

וכל דבר ניבול וצד דבר ערווה לא ישמע על פיך, כגון להזכיר זונה או כל דבר נבלה כי - שוחה[86] עמוקה פי זרות. מעמיקים[87] לו גיהנם. והופכים לו גזר דין של שבעים שנה לרעה. ואף השומעים ושותקים ונהנים בשמיעה ואינם הולכים משם, נכשלים בדבר.

And any lascivious talk or kind of sexually immoral speech shall not be heard upon your mouth, such as mentioning a prostitute or any obscene thing. For - The mouth of a forbidden woman is a deep pit. These deepen **Gehinnom**[hell] for him and it is appropriate that he should be liable for a divine decree of seventy years for punishment. And even those who hear and are silent but enjoy hearing and do not leave from there come to grief on the matter.

ואל תחשוד חברך, כי שמא כשר הוא בדבר, והחושד[88] בכשרים לוקה בגופו.

Do not suspect your fellow, since he may be

---

[85] מועד קטן כא ב
[86] משלי כב יד
[87] שבת לג א
[88] יומא יט ב

Sefer HaYirah   ספר היראה

worthy in the thing, and one who suspects the worthy is smitten with disease.

ואל תביא עצמך לידי חשד, להיות נקי מה' ומישראל, פן ייכשלו בני אדם על ידך שיחשדוך הבריות. מחול לכל החושדים בך.

And do not bring yourself into suspicion, being clean from God and from Israel, lest people should come to grief by your hand, since God's creations suspected you. Pardon all who suspect you.

ואל[89] תהרוג כינה, ואל תעשה שום דבר מאוס בפני חברך.

Do not kill a louse or do a single loathsome thing in front of your fellow.

ואם עשו אחרים לפניך ונמאסת, מחול להם ואל ייכשלו על ידך.

But if others do so in front of you and you were filled with loathing pardon them that they should not come to grief by your hand.

ואם מצאת רוק מוטל, הרם וסלקהו או כסהו ומחול לאשר עשה אותו, פן יבוא אחר ויכשילנו שלא ימחול.

If you have found spittle lying on the ground, pick it up and take it away or cover it, and forgive whoever did it, in case another should come and it cause him to come to grief since he shall not forgive

והזהר שלא ימצא טינוף על בגדיך או שומן או כל דבר

---

[89] חגיגה ה א

Sefer HaYirah ספר היראה

מאוס, כי המתלכלך ואינו נזהר בנקיות, משניא אוהביו של מקום לבריות וחייב מיתה, שנאמר - כל[90] משנאי אהבו מות. אל[91] תקרי משנאי אלא משניאי. ויראי השם שאינם משמרים עצמם בנקיות, אומרים רואיהם, כמה לומדי תורה מאוסים, ונמצא שם שמים מתחלל על ידיהם.

And take care that filth shall not be found upon your clothes or fat, or any loathsome thing. For one who soils himself and is not careful with cleanliness causes the lovers of God, the divine creations to hate and is worthy of the death penalty. As is said - All they who hate me love death. Do not read **M'sanai** [Those who hate me], they who hate, but rather **Mas'ni'ai** [Those who cause me to be hated], they who cause hate. And people who see God fearers who do not keep themselves in cleanliness say - How many learners of Torah are filthy! and the result is - the Name of Heaven is desecrated by them.

ואל תשקץ נפשך בהשהות נקביך, והמשהה נקביו בגדולים ובקטנים, עובר בשתים - אל[92] תשקצו. ולא יראה בך ערות דבר.[93]

Do not make your soul detestable by delaying your openings. The one who delays his openings in the large and in the small transgresses two negative commandments - You shall not make yourselves abominable. and - That He see no unclean thing in you.

---

[90] משלי ח לו
[91] שבת קיד א
[92] ויקרא יא מג
[93] דברים כג טו

ספר היראה / Sefer HaYirah

אל תאמר שום נחוש, כי[94] לא נחש ביעקב ולא קסם בישראל. ובכמה מקומות הזהירה תורתנו - לא[95] ימצא בך מעביר בנו ובתו באש קסם קסמים מעונן ומנחש ומכשף. לא[96] תנחשו. ואין לנו לשים שום סימן אלא מה שאמרו חכמינו זיכרונם לברכה, ואם יש לו לאדם לעשות מצווה, כגון לחזור על מסכתא או להשיב בנו אל הספר, לא יאמר אמתין עד ראש חדש או עד הפסח, כי בכל יום ובכל עת, טוב להתחיל ולעשות מצוות, ומי שאינו מקפיד, לעולם לא יקפידו עמו, אך המקפידים, השטן עומד על ימינם ולהחזיקם בטעותם.

You shall not say a word of soothsaying, for - Lo, there is no augury in YAACOV, no divining in Israel. In how many places does our Torah warn - There shall not be found among you…or a soothsayer - You shall not practice divination or soothsaying. And we are not to make any sign but only what our sages of blessed memory have said. And if a person has to do a mitzvah such as to return to the tractate of the Talmud or to make his son return to the book, he should not say - I shall wait until the new moon or until Pesach. For every day and at every time it is good to begin to do mitzvot. And, one who does not lose his temper - They should never lose their tempers with him. But the ones who lose their tempers - The Accuser stands upon their right and their left, strengthening them in their error.

---

[94] במדבר כג כג
[95] דברים יח י
[96] ויקרא יט כו

Sefer HaYirah   ספר היראה

אל תתכבד בקלון חברך.

Do not elevate yourself at the expense of the degradation of your fellow.

ואל תרים זרועך על שום אדם להכותו, כי הסוטר לועו של ישראל, כאלו סוטר לועו של שכינה, שנאמר - מוקש[97] אדם ילע קדש.

And you shall not raise your arm against any man to strike him, for the one who slaps a Jew's face is as if he slaps the face of the **Shekhinah** [The presence of God], as is said - It is a snare for a man to rashly declare it is holy.

ותקצץ ידו, שנאמר - וזרוע[98] רמה תשבר.

And his hand be cut off. As is said - The upraised arm is broken.

וראוי הוא להיקבר חי, שנאמר - ואיש[99] זרוע לו הארץ.

And he is fitting to be buried alive, as is said - The mighty man, who has the earth.

ואפילו בהרמת[100] יד נקרא רשע, שנאמר - ויאמר[101] לרשע למה תכה רעך.

And even when he raises his hand, he is called wicked, as in - He said to the wicked one, why do you smite your fellow

על כן יש לו לאדם להיזהר מאוד מלהכות, אם לא בנו הקטן

---

[97] משלי כ כה
[98] איוב לח טו
[99] איוב כח ח
[100] סנהדרין נח ב
[101] שמות ב יג

Sefer HaYirah

או תלמידו שהוא מוכיחו.
Therefore, a person must take much care to avoid striking, if it is not his minor child or his student who he is rebuking.

אם[102] תוכיח את חברך, אל תוכיחנו ויתבייש, אבל תוכיחנו בסתר. ואפילו מאה פעמים.
If you shall rebuke your fellow do not rebuke him and put him to shame, but rebuke him in secret. Even a hundred times.

אל תלבין פני חברך ברבים, כי המלבין פני חברו, דם יחשב לו דם שפך. תדע, דאזיל סומקא ואתי חוורא, ואין לו חלק לעולם הבא. ונוח[103] לו לאדם שיפיל עצמו לתוך כבשן האש ואל ילבין פני חברו ברבים.
You shall not whiten the face of your fellow in public, for one who whitens his fellow's face, it is considered blood, spilled blood, as you know - the red color of the face disappears and the white takes its place and he has no share in the world to come. And it would be better for that man that he should throw himself down into a fiery furnace than to whiten his fellow's face in public.

אך אם הוכח הוכחת אדם בסתר כמה פעמים ולא קבל, מותר לביישו ולהלבין פניו ולשנאתו ולרודפו עד שיקבל. וכל מי שיש בידו להוכיח ואינו מוכיח אדם עובר, העברה בראשו. ואם הוכיח, אז נפשו הציל.
But if you have strongly rebuked a person in

---

[102] ערכין טז ב
[103] ברכות מג ב

Sefer HaYirah

private a few times but he does not accept it, it is permitted to put him to shame and whiten his face and hate him and pursue him until he does accept it. And anyone who is in a position to rebuke the one who commits a transgression but does not rebuke the transgressor, the transgression is on his head. But if he does rebuke, then it saves his life.

Sefer HaYirah ספר היראה

נשים Women

אל¹⁰⁴ תתייחד עם שום אישה, אפילו בתך או אחותך, ואפילו פנויה. חוץ מאשתך - ואפילו היא נדה, ואימך.
Do not be alone with any woman, even your daughter or your sister, and even an unmarried woman, other than your wife, even if she is ritually impure due to menstruation and your mother.

ואיזהו יחוד. סגור במפתח או במנעול, זהו ייחוד האמור בתורה - כי¹⁰⁵ יסיתך אחיך בן אמך וגו'.
Now what does it mean to be alone. To be in a room locked with a key or with a padlock, this is being alone as said in the Torah - If your brother the son of your mother or your son or your daughter or the wife of your bosom entices you in secret.

ואפילו עם שתי נשים.
And even with two women.

וטוב ליזהר אפילו בפתח פתוח לרשות הרבים, משבת עם אישה אחת.
And it is good to be on guard against even sitting with one woman in an open doorway in public.

אל¹⁰⁶ תשמיע לאוזנך במתכון קול אישה משוררת, כי קול

---

¹⁰⁴ קידושין פא ב
¹⁰⁵ דברים יג ז
¹⁰⁶ ברכות כד א

ספר היראה | Sefer HaYirah

באישה ערווה. שערה וכל האמור בשיר[107] השירים, ערווה. קול, שער, שנים, צוואר, כל האמור בפרשה לשבח.

Do not let your ears hear the voice of a woman singing, for the voice of a woman is nakedness, her hair is nakedness, and everything that is mentioned in Song of Songs voice, hair, teeth, neck is nakedness.

ואסור[108] לו להסתכל אפילו באצבע קטנה של אישה, לזון עיניו מן הערווה. וכל המרצה מעות לאישה מידו לידה כדי להסתכל בה, אפילו קיבל תורה כמשה רבנו מידו של הקדוש ברוך הוא, לא ינקה מדינה של גיהנם.

And it is forbidden for him even to gaze at the little finger of a woman to derive pleasure from the sight. And anyone who pays money to a woman by counting coins from his hand to her hand in order to gaze at her, even though he might have received the Torah at Sinai like our Teacher Moses from the hand of the Holy One Blessed be He, will not be cleared from the sentence of Gehinnom[hell].

הרגל תמיד שפתיך דברי יראת שמים, כגון - הוי[109] עז כנמר. סוף[110] דבר הכל נשמע. ועתה ישראל מה ה' אלוהיך שאל מעמך כי אם ליראה[111] וגו'. מאוד[112] מאוד הוי שפל-רוח. וכיוצא באלה, הרגל על לשונך, ואז לא תיכשל.

---

[107] שיר השירים ז ב-י
[108] ברכות כד א
[109] פרקי אבות ה כ
[110] קהלת יב יג
[111] דברים י יב
[112] פרקי אבות ד ד

Sefer HaYirah סֵפֶר הַיִרְאָה

אל תהדוק ראשך על הספר.
Do not be attached to a book.

ואל תהרוג כינה על השולחן, כי הוא נקרא מזבח. ואל תדבר בשעת ברכת המזון.
Nor kill a louse on the table, for it is called an altar. And do not speak during the Grace after Meals.

גדל בניך לתלמוד תורה ולמעשים טובים, גם לעת זקנה לא יסורו.
Bring up your sons for learning Torah and good deeds, even in their old age they will not depart from them.

ולמד לבנותיך הלכות נדה וחלה, איסור והתר דברים הנוהגים בהן, פן יאכילוך דבר אסור או לבני ביתן.
And teach your daughters the laws of **Nidah** [Family Purity] and separating **Challah** [the law of Kneading and baking bread], prohibitions and what permitted, teachings that apply to them lest they feed you a forbidden thing or to the members of their families.

הוי זהיר בברכת הלבנה בכל חודש בזמנה, משיאותו לאורה ועד רובו של חודש, כי - אלמלי[113] לא זכו ישראל אלא להקביל פני אביהם שבשמים בכל חודש וחודש, דים.
Take be careful in reciting the blessing of the New Moon each month, at its proper time from when they enjoy its light until the fullness of the moon. For if Israel were to merit nothing

---
[113] סנהדרין מב א

Sefer HaYirah

but to greet their Father in heaven only once a month, it would be enough for them.

הוי זהיר בכבוד אשתך, כדברי רבותינו, אוהב[114] אשתו כגופו ומכבדה יותר מגופו. כי[115] דייך שהיא מגדלת בניך ומצלת עצמך מן החטא.

Take care with the honor due your wife, according to our sages - He loves his wife as himself, and honors her more than himself. For it is enough for you that she raises your children and saves you from sin.

והוי[116] זהיר באונאתה, כי דמעתה מצויה, לפיכך אונאתה מצויה וקרובה, כי שערי דמעה לא ננעלו.

And be careful not to hurt her feelings, for her tears are frequent. Therefore, her pain is immanent, for the gates of tears are not locked.

הסתר סודך, וכל שכן סוד אחרים. משוכבת[117] חיקך שמור פתחי פיך.

Keep your secret and all the more so with another's secret. As it says - Keep the gates of your mouth shut from her that lies in your bosom.

התנאה במצוות כפי כוחך, והידור[118] מצווה עד שליש במצווה. כגון, מצא אתרוג בשתים עשרה פרוטות, ומצא אחר הדור ממנו, יוסיף עד שמונה עשרה פרוטות לקחת

---

[114] יבמות סב ב
[115] יבמות סג א
[116] בבא מציעא נט א
[117] מיכה ז ה
[118] בבא קמא ט ב

Sefer HaYirah   ספר הִיראה

את ההדור.

Enjoy the **Mitzvot** to the most of your ability. And adorn the Mitzvah up to one third of the value of the mitzvah. For example, if he found an etrog for 12 **Prutas** [A small coin of money] and he found another one more beautiful than it, he should add up to 18 Prutas to get the more beautiful one.

מצווה שאין לה דורש, תידרשנה. ואל[119] תהי קלה בעיניך לא מצווה ולא עברה.

A mitzvah that has no interpretation: interpret it. And let it not be a light thing in your eyes, neither the mitzvah, nor the transgression.

ואל תברח מעשות מצווה לא בשביל יראת הפסד ולא מפני פחד עונש הגוף, כי כדאית היא המצווה לשומרך מכל היזק. ואם חס וחלילה יארע לך היזק, נאמן הוא בעל מלאכתך שימלא חסרונך שחסרת בעבורו.

You shall not flee from doing a mitzvah neither for fear of monetary loss nor because of fear of physical pain. For the mitzvah is worth it to protect you from all danger. And if, God forbid, some damages should befall you, the master of your labor is faithful to repay the loss that you incurred on its behalf.

---

[119] פרקי אבות ד ב

ספר הי'ראה   Sefer HaYirah

בדרך On the way

בצאתך לדרך צא בכי טוב, והיזהר בתפלת הדרך. וזו היא - יהי רצון מלפניך ה' אלוהי"ו ואלוה"י אבותינו, שתוליכנו לשלום, ותצעידנו לשלום, ותסמכנו לשלום, ותצילנו מכף כל אויב ואורב בדרך, ותנחנו אל מחוז חפצנו בשלום, ותחזירנו לבתינו לשלום, כי אתה שומע תפלה, ברוך אתה ה', שומע תפלה.

When you go on your way, go without any harm being done. And take care with reciting the Wayfarer's Prayer, and this is it - May it be your will, our god and God of our fathers, that you lead us in safety and direct us in safety, and support us in peace. And that you save us from the hand of all foes and those lyings-in wait on the road. And may you bring us to rest to the safe harbor of our desire in peace, and may you return us to our homes in peace, for you are the One who hears prayer. Blessed are You, the eternal, who hears prayer.

וצריך לאומרה אפילו אם אינו רוצה ללכת אלא פרסה, ובתוך מהלך פרסה. וכן אם שכח לאמרה ונזכר לאחר שהלך פרסה, אומר בלא חתימת ברכה.

And he must say it even if he does not want to go, except if he is only going a **Parasang** [Distance mentioned in the Talmud, about 3.7 kilometer]. And he must say it within walking a parasang. And the same if he forgot to say it and remembered after walking more than a parasang, but he says it without the seal of the blessing.

ספר הִיִראה · Sefer HaYirah

פגעת גויים, אל תשנה דבורך כאלו **אינך יהודי**. גם אם יאמרו לך **גוי אתה**, אמור **יהודי אני**.

If gentiles confront you do not change your manner of speaking as if you were **not a Jew**. Even if they say to you - **You are a gentile**, say to them - **I am a Jew**.

ולא תעבור על המוכסנין ותיתפש ותשים יראתך ונפשך על קרן הצבי. אל תעמוד במקום סכנה ותסמוך על הנס, אך תירא תמיד פן יגרום החטא. וזכור ליעקב אבינו - וייראַ[120] יעקב מאד ויצר לו.

And do not cross the toll-collectors and get arrested and put your dignity and your life at risk. You shall not stand in a place of danger and rely upon a miracle, but always fear lest it cause you to sin. But remember our father Yaakov - Then Yaakov was greatly afraid and distressed. Do not annoy even a gentile child for the gentiles bear grudges.

אל תקניט גוי קטן, כי הגויים נוטרי איבה הם.

Do not tease a small gentile, for the Gentiles are notorious for hostility.

אל תהי צדיק הרבה - ראית אישה טובעת בנהר, אל תאמר אנוס ולא אראנה, וכיוצא בזה, שמעת איש אומר להכות את חברו, אל תאמר, לא אגלה לו ואהיה רכיל - לא[121] תעמוד על דם רעך, ואמור לו כפי יכולתך שלא בלשון רכילות, ואז את נפשך הצלת.

Do not be too righteous. If you see a naked

---

[120] בראשית לב ח
[121] ויקרא יט טז

Sefer HaYirah ספר היראה

woman drowning in a river, do not say - I shall flee and I shall not look at her, or things like this. If you hear a man saying he will kill his fellow, do not say - I shall not reveal him and be a talebearer. Do not stand by the blood of your neighbor, but say to the best of your ability that it is not the language of talebearing, and then your life shall be saved.

אל תשבח אישה ביופייה בפני חברך, פן על ידך יחמדנה, וכתיב - לא[122] תחמד. קרי בה לא תחמיד, וכן קרי בה לא תחמוד.

Do not praise a woman for her beauty in front of your fellow, lest you should make him desire her, when the verse - You shall not covet. can be read - You shall not covet. and also, be read - You shall not cause coveting.

אל תקשט עצמך ותלך בין הנשים כדי שיתאוו לך.

Do not flirt with the women in order to seize them with desire for you.

ואל[123] תרבה שיחה עימהן, אפילו עם אשתך.

And do not increase conversation with them, even with your wife.

וזה ריבוי שיחה, כאותו[124] ששאל לברוריה **באיזו דרך נלך ללוד**, אמרה לו, גלילי שוטה, היה לך לומר, **באיזו ללוד**.

Now this is increase of conversation, like the

---

[122] שמות כ טז
[123] פרקי אבות א ה
[124] עירובין נג ב

Sefer HaYirah   ספר היראה

one that asked of **Beruriah** [the wife of Rabbi Meir] - By **which road do we go to Lod**. She said to him - Stupid Galilean! You should have asked me - **which to Lod**.

ולא יעיין בבגדי-צבע שלהן, ואפילו שטוחים על הכותל.
Nor should he look at their dyed clothes, even those stretched out on the wall to dry.

כללו של דבר, כל מה שיוכל להתרחק מהן וממשאן וממתנן ומדיבורן, יתרחק, כי[125] תמיד יצר הרע בוער כאש להחטיא את האדם, ולכן צריך האדם להיות כל שעה יועץ תחבולות לעשות מלחמה עמו.
The rule of the matter: whatever a man can do to distance himself from women and their business transactions and their speech, he should do to distance himself. For the evil inclination is forever burning like a fire to cause man to sin. Therefore, a man must always be a military advisor to make war with the evil inclination.

אל[126] תשבח אדם בפני שונאו שמתקנא בו, ומתוך שבחו בא לידי גנותו. ואל תגנהו בפני אוהבו.
Do not praise anyone in front of his enemy, since it makes him incensed against him and in the praise cause him to speak of his shortcomings, and do not put him to shame in front of his friend.

---

[125] קידושין ל ב
[126] ערכין טז ב

Sefer HaYirah ספר היראה

אל תגנה מיקח חברו בפניו ואל תשבחהו, אלא שתוק, כי למה תשב ותחניף.
Do not censure the bargain of your fellow in front of him, and do not praise him but rather be silent; why would you respond and flatter.

אל[127] תכנס לביתך פתאום, וכל שכן לבית חברך.
Do not enter your home suddenly, and all the more so for your neighbor's house.

אל תייעץ אדם לפי דרכך, אלא תן עצה טובה והוגנת לכל מי שייוועץ אתך לכבוד הבורא.
Do not advise a person according to your way, but rather give advice that is good and befitting to whomever seeks counsel with you, for the honor of the Creator.

כללו של דבר, כל[128] דבר המסור לליבך, שאין אדם מבחין למה אתה מתכוון, לטובה או לרעה, נאמר בו - ויראת[129] מאלוהיך. המכיר מחשבתך.
The rule of the matter, anything that is entrusted to your heart that a person cannot distinguish for what you intend, whether for good or for evil, on this it is said - You shall fear your God. the One who knows your thoughts.

אל תקרא שום אדם בכינויו, אפילו שלא בפניו, ואפילו לומר לאדם כדי שיוכל להכירו, אך דחוק עצמך בעניין

---

[127] פסחים קיב א
[128] בבא מציעא נח ב
[129] ויקרא יט יד

Sefer HaYirah   ספר הִירִאָה

אחר פלוני בן פלוני עד שיכירהו.

Do not call any man by his attribute, even if he is not in front of you, or even to say it to a nether person so that he may be able to recognize him. Rather push yourself after what that person is really about until he can recognize him.

אל תקרא לשום אדם בשום דבר ניוול, ואפילו לקטן אסור לקרותו מאוס דרך שחוק, כי כולם נקיים וקדושים.

Do not call any one by the name of any disgraceful thing; it is forbidden to call even a child by any loathsome or repulsive name in a joking manner for they are all clean and holy.

ואל תשבח שום גוי לא בחן ולא ביפי ולא במעשיו.

And do not praise any gentile neither by grace, nor by beauty, but rather by his deeds.

וכשתראה[130] גוי עשה טובה או נאמנות או צדקה, דאג, כי חסד[131] לאומים חטאת לישראל, ואל תדינם לכף זכות אם לא בפניהם מפני דרכי שלום.

And when you see a gentile doing good, or righteousness, or dealing faithfully worry, for grace for the nations of the world is sin for Israel. And do not give them the benefit of the doubt except in front of them for the sake of peace.

ואל תיתן דיו לסופרי אומות העולם הכותבים שמות

---

[130] בבא בתרא י ב
[131] משלי יד לד

ספר היראה Sefer HaYirah

הטומאה ופסליהם, כי אסור לסייע ידי עוברי עברה.

Do not give ink to gentile scribes who write the Names of impurity and its nullities for it is forbidden to support the hands of transgressors.

הישמר[132] מלצער בעלי חיים, הן בהמה הן עוף, וכל שכן שלא לצער אדם, שהוא עשוי בצלם המקום.

Be on guard against causing pain to animals, whether beast or foul, and all the more so not to cause pain to a person, since he is made in the image of the Omnipresent One.

אם אתה רוצה לשכור פועלים ומצאת עניים, יהיו עניים בני ביתך, ואך אל תבזה אותם, אך דרך כבוד תצווה להם, ותשלם שכרם מושלם, ואל תדחם בלך ושוב, כי הרבה לאוין יש בדבר, ואליו הוא נושא את נפשו.

If you want to hire workers and you have found poor ones, let them be as members of your own family. And you shall surely not disdain them, you shall only command them in a manner of respect, and pay them their wages in full, neither shall you press them in saying, **Go and come Back**, for there are many negative commandments about the matter and to it He may take his life in payment.

אל תשב בין העומדים ואל תעמוד בין היושבים, ולא תישן בין הערים ואל תהי ער בין הישנים, ולא שמח בין העצבים ולא עצב בין השמחים.

Do not sit among the standing nor stand among the sitting; do not sleep among the waking nor

---

[132] בבא מציעא לב ב

Sefer HaYirah ספר היראה

be awake among the sleeping. Do not rejoice among the sorrowful nor be sorrowful among those who rejoice.

כללו[133] של דבר, אל ישנה אדם מן המנהג, אך הכל יהיה לטובה וביראת שמים, שאם רואה לצים, אל יתלוצץ כמותם.

The rule of the matter - a person should not differ from the custom; however, all will be for good and fear of heaven if one should see scoffers, he shall not join in their scoffer.

אל תתפאר משום דבר שעשית.

Do not be glorified by any thing that you have done.

ואף אל תעמוד במקום שיש מעלה, פן יגבה לבבך.

Do not even stand in a place where there is superior rank lest your heart grow haughty.

ואם שמעת ששיבחוך בני אדם, דאג והצטער בדבר.

Now if you hear that people have praised you, worry and apologize about the matter.

אל תפרוש מן הצבור, כי לא תקבל שכר עמהם.

Do not separate yourself from the community, for you shall not receive a reward with them.

ואם תפרוש, שני[134] מלאכים המלווים לו לאדם מניחים ידיהם על ראשו ואומרים, פלוני שפרש מן הצבור, אל

---

[133] עיין כריתות יז א
[134] תענית יא א

Sefer HaYirah

יראה בנחמת הצבור.

And if you separate, the two accompanying angels that every person has set their hands upon his head and say - **So-and-so**, who separated from the community, shall not see the comfort of that community.

אם מינוך צבור פרנס, אל תתגאה עליהם.

If the community has elected you leader, do not lord it over them.

ואל[135] תטיל עליהם אימה שלא לשם שמים, וסבול טורחם, כי גדול פרנס הדור.

And do not put fear over them that is not for the sake of heaven. And bear their troubles, for the reward of a great leader of the generation.

ואם אתה סופר, אל[136] תחסר אות או תיבה, או תייתר לחתום שמך בראש.

Now, if you are a Torah scribe, do not omit a letter or a word or add to sign your name at the top.

אם אתה שכיר ללמד תורה, הזהר בשעת מלאכתך מלעשות מלאכה אחרת, אף לא שום דבר, כי ברגע יטעו תלמידיך ולא תשמע, ומלאכתך מלאכת רמיה, ורמיה בארור. ואף לא לענות ולדבר לשום אדם, ולמד[137] מאבא חלקיה זכרונו לברכה.

And if you are hired to teach Torah, take care

---

[135] ראש השנה יז א
[136] עירובין יג א
[137] תענית כג א

Sefer HaYirah   ספר היראה

when you are at your work not to do any other work, not even any other thing, for the moment your students shall err but you shall not hear, your work is a work of cheating, and cursed chearting. Not even to answer or speak to anyone, and learn from **Abba Hilkiyah**, of blessed memory.

אל תשכן באהיליך ספר חומש נביאים וכתובים, שאינו מוגה אם ידעת להגיהו.
There shall not dwell in your home a book of Torah, Prophets, and Writings that has not been corrected if you know how to correct it.

ואל[138] תניח ביתך בלא מעקה למדרגות.
And do not allow your home to be without a railing for the steps.

ואל[139] תגדל כלב רע או שום מזיק.
Nor shall you raise a dangerous dog or anything else that causes damage in the midst of your home.

כללו של דבר, הסר מביתך כל הזק וכל מכשול.
The rule of the matter - remove from your home every danger and every stumbling block.

שאלת כלי מחברך או כל דבר לעשות בו מלאכה, אל תעשה בו מלאכה אחרת.
If you have borrowed a tool from your

---

[138] דברים כב ח
[139] בבא קמא טו ב

Sefer HaYirah ספר היראה

neighbor, or anything else with which to do work, do not do other work with it.

ואל תשאל שום דבר שלא ברשות, כי[140] השואל שלא מדעת, גזלן הוא.

You shall not borrow any thing without permission, for one who borrows without knowledge is a robber.

ואל[141] תשאיל לאחרים, בלא רשות מי ששאלת ממנו.

And do not lend it to others without permission from whom you borrowed it.

ואם[142] נתן לך אדם דבר להשתמש בו, אל תמכרנו שלא ברשותו. או אם נתן לך דמים לקח טלית, אל תיקח בהם חלוק, כי המשנה מדעת בעל הבית, גזלן הוא.

If a person has given you something to use, do not sell it without his permission. Or if he has given you payment to buy a tallit katan do not buy an undershirt with it, for the one who deviates from the consent of the master of the house is a robber.

כלל גדול בתורה - דעלך[143] סני, לחברך לא תעבד.

The greatest rule in the Torah - That which is hateful to you, do not due to your neighbor.

וכל עת וכל שעה חשוב איך תעשה מצות ואיך תשמר מעברה, כדי שתשלים כל היום בטובה.

---

[140] בבא בתרא פח א
[141] בבא מציעא כט א
[142] בבא מציעא עח ב
[143] שבת לא א

Sefer HaYirah ספר הירְאָה

At every time and every hour, it is important how you shall do the commandments and how you shall keep from transgression in order that you should finish the entire day with goodness.

סוף[144] דבר הכל נשמע. הסר מלבך כל מחשבות און, אך הרהור תורה ויראת שמים.

The end of the matter when all is said and done. remove from your heart all thoughts of iniquity, only meditation on Torah and fear of Heaven.

ובמקום מטונף בבית הכסא, יחשוב חשבונות, וזה הדבר יסיר מליבו מחשבות טהורות במקום טינופת.

And instead of being soiled in the bathroom let him think of Will calculate accounts. for this is the thing that will remove from his heart thoughts of pollution and replace them with thoughts of purity.

ואחרי טהרתו, ישוב למחשבתו הראשונה, איך יהיה זהיר בעבודת הבורא, וזה נקרא ערום ביראה.

And after his purity let him return to his prior thoughts, how he should be strict in the service of the Creator, this one is called deliberate in the fear of God.

---

[144] קהלת יב יג

Sefer HaYirah   ספר הַיִראה

In the evening לעת ערב

לעת ערב לך ובדוק עצמך יפה יפה, טרם שתלך לבית התפלה.

At evening time go and examine yourself exceedingly well before you walk to the synagogue.

ולבש מכנסיך ועשה כל הסדר שאמרנו בתפלת שחרית.

Put on your pants and do the entire order which we have said with regard to the morning prayers.

ואם תוכל, לא תאכל לא בימות החמה ולא בימות הגשמים עד לאחר תפלת הערב, כמו שדרשו רבותינו[145] - ואותי[146] השלכת אחרי גוך. לאחר שנתגאית תקבל עול מלכות שמים, אם לא תאכל בעוד היום גדול שיעור שלש פרסאות.

Now, if you are able, you shall not eat before the evening prayer, neither on days of heat nor on days of rain, as our sages, may their memory be for a blessing, expounded in from the verse - And me, you have cast behind your back. for after you become haughty shall you accept the Kingdom of God. If you do not eat for the rest of the day the measure increases threefold.

בא מבית התפלה והגיע זמן שכיבה, יקרא קריאת שמע כולה שיש בה מאתים וארבעים ושמונה תיבות, להרחיק כל מזיק ממאתיים וארבעים ושמונה אברים שבו. ויהי[147] נעם, והשכיבנו בלא חתימה. ומקראות, אחד המרבה ואחד הממעיט, ויפקיד רוחו ביד בוראו, ויתוודה, וימחול לכל

---

[145] ברכות י ב
[146] מלכים-א יד ט
[147] תהלים צ יז

Sefer HaYirah   ספר הֵירְאָה

המצערים אותו, כדאמרי רבותינו - שרי[148] לה לכל מאן דמצערן.

If he has come from the house of prayer and the time for bed has come, let him recite all of the **S'hma** since there are two hundred forty-eight words in it to keep all danger away from the two hundred forty-eight limbs in him. And let him say the - **Vihi n'oam** [After reading Shema Yisrael], and the **Hashkivenu** [Let us lie down] without a **Chatimah** [with out the name of God]. And let him recite verses of Torah - One great, and One small. Then let him commend his soul to the hand of his Creator. Then let him confess and forgive all who hurt him, according to the sages of our sages may their memory be for a blessing - Let him forgive for all the hurts they may do him.

וייתן מיטתו בין צפון לדרום.
Let him put his bed between north to south.

ויחלוץ נעל של שמאל, ואחר כך של ימין.
Then let him take off his left shoe first, and afterwards his right shoe.

וישכב, ויסיר חלוקו במיטתו, ולא יראוהו קורות ביתו מגולה. ואם יש שם כתבי קודש במקום אשר הוא שוכב שם, יכסה. וחומש, צריך להניח בתיבה, ומכוסה.
Then let him lie down and take off his undershirt in his bed without the beams of his house seeing him naked. And if he has holy

---

[148] מגילה כח א

Sefer HaYirah

writings there in the place where he sleeps let him cover them. And as for a **Chumash** [Torah] he must set it down in a chest and it must be covered.

ואל יישן פרקדן, פן ישים ידו על הערווה.
Now he must not sleep lying on his back in case he should place his hand upon the nakedness.

ואם יש לו אישה, יהיה צנוע, ויזהר מדבר עמה נבלה, כי אף שיחה בטלה שבין איש לאשתו, על[149] הכל בא במשפט.
And if he has a wife, he should be modest and strict not to speak with her obscenely, for even idle chatter that is between a man and his wife, all of it is judged.

ובשעת בעילה, אל יהרהר באישה אחרת, כי כמעט עושה בניו ממזרים.
And during intercourse he must not fantasize about another woman for it nearly makes his children bastards.

ואל יאכוף אשתו לדבר מצווה, אלא יפייסנה.
He must not force his wife in the matter of a mitzvah, rather he should persuade her.

ואל ישמש עמה סמוך לוסתה עונה אחת, ולא ביום.
Nor should he couple with her half the day before her regular date of menstruation, and not on the day of it.

---

[149] קהלת יב יד

Sefer HaYirah   ספר היראה

ויזהר מאוד מאוד שלא יוציא שום נבול ודבר ערווה מפיו אף דרך שחוק.
He should be exceedingly careful that no obscenity or word of immorality come out of his mouth, even by way of a joke.

ויתכוון בשעת מעשה, לשם מצווה, ושיהיו לו בנים שילכו בדרכי השם, ולא יתכוון להנאתו.
Let him intend when doing the deed that it be for the sake of a mitzvah, that he should have children who will walk in the ways of the Lord, let him not intend to enjoy it.

ויזהר כפי יכולתו שלא יוציא זרע לבטלה.
And let him avoid wanton emission of seed to the best of his ability.

וקדם שישכב, ילמד, לקים מצות - והגית[150] בו יומם ולילה, וישכב ויישן וינוח.
Before retiring, he should study Torah to fulfill the Mitzvah of - You shall meditate upon it day and night. The he should lie down and sleep and rest.

הנה כל הסדר הזה ינהג כל ימי הבלו, ועוד יוסיף כהנה וכהנה לעשות טובה ויראת שמים.
Why, let a man be guided by this entire order as long as he breathes and let him add like this and like that to do good and increase the fear of God.

---

[150] יהושע א ח

Sefer HaYirah   ספר הׄיראה

שבת Sabbath

וישלים[151] פרשיותיו עם הצבור בכל שבוע, שנים מקרא ואחד תרגום.

Let him complete his weekly Torah portions with the community, twice in the original and once in Translating of **Onkelos** [Aramaic] translation.

ואם אין לו תרגום, יקרא שנים מקרא ואחד לעז.

But if he does not have an Aramaic translation he may read twice in the original and once in the vernacular.

וטוב יותר מלומר שלוש פעמים המקרא, כי התרגום היה להבין המקרא למי שאינו בקי, כל שכן לעז פרוש שהיא לשון הלועזות.

Which is even better than reading three times in the original for the Aramaic translation was for one who was not well versed, how much the more so is the vernacular commentary for those who speak the vernacular.

והמקרא[152] יקרא בנגינותיו, כי הקורא בלא זמרה, התורה חוגרת שק.

Now, let him chant the Torah with its tropes, for if one reads it without its melody, the Torah puts on sackcloth.

ובערב שבת, יטרח לסעודת שבת. ואפילו יש לו כמה

---

[151] ברכות ח א
[152] סנהדרין קא א

Sefer HaYirah   ספר היראה

עבדים, יטרח הוא בעצמו לכבוד שבת הנקראת כלה ומלכה, ושקולה כנגד כל המצות.

And on the eve of the Sabbath, he should prepare for the Sabbath meal. And even if he has several servants, he should prepare it by himself for the honor of the Sabbath, which is called 'Bride and 'Queen and its value is equal to all the other Mitzvot on the scale.

וישתדל בתיקוני שבת, כי[153] הא דרבא מלח שבוטא.

And let him strive to complete Sabbath preparations for this is the thing - Raba salted a **Shibbuta** [A type of fish found in the rivers of Baghdad] himself for the Sabbath.

ולפי כוחו יקנה מעדנים לענג שבת.

And as much as he can, let him buy sweets for the joy of the Sabbath.

ולא[154] יאכל בערב שבת מן המנחה ולמעלה, פן יפסיד סעודת שבת.

He should not eat on Sabbath eve from **Minchah** [afternoon] onwards, in case he should spoil the Sabbath evening meal.

וסמוך לערב יערוך[155] שולחן, כסא ומנורה, ויכין הכל, כוסות וקערות.

And right before evening he should set the table, chair and candelabra and put all of the

---

[153] שבת קיט א
[154] גיטין לח ב
[155] מלכים-ב ד י

Sefer HaYirah ספר היראה

cups and dishes in their proper place.

ויהיה[156] זהיר ליין לקדוש היום.
And let him be strict with the wine for the Sanctification of the Day.

וייטול ציפורניו בכל ערב שבת.
He should cut his fingernails every Sabbath eve.

וישחיז סכינו, כמו שדרשו רבותינו - והיה[157] ביום השישי והכינו את. - זה השחזת סכין.
And he should sharpen his knife, as our sages expounded - On the sixth day when they shall prepare. this means sharpening the knife.

ועוד דרשו - וידעת[158] כי שלום אהלך. - זה השחזת סכין, כי אם קהה הברזל ולא יוכל לחתוך, אין זה שלום בית.
They further expounded - You shall know that your tent is at peace, this means the sharpening of the knife, for if the knife is dull and will not cut this is not fulfilling the commandment of peace of the home.

וירחץ[159] פניו ידיו ורגליו בחמין לערב אחר שעשה כל צרכיו.
Then he should wash his face, his hands, and his feet with hot water for the evening after he has done all his needs.

---

[156] פסחים קו ב
[157] שמות טז ה
[158] איוב ה כד
[159] שבת כה ב

Sefer HaYirah סֵפֶר הַיִרְאָה

וכל מה שיעשה, יחשוב לעשות לכבוד שבת.
Everything that he may do, let him think to do it for the honor of the Sabbath.

ויוסיף מחול על הקודש.
Then let him add from the profane up to the holy.

ועם חשכה, ימשמש בבגדיו, וידליק בעוד השמש בראש האילנות.
With onset of darkness let him examine his clothes and let him light candles while the sun is still upon the top of the trees.

קידש היום, יתפלל של שבת, וינוח ויתענג, ויסיר מליבו כל אנחה וכל מחשבה, כאלו כל מלאכתו עשויה.
He sanctifies the day and he should pray the order of prayers of the Sabbath; then he should rest and enjoy himself. And he should banish from his heart all groaning and all thoughts, as if all his work were done.

ויכבד את השבת בכסות נקיה ושולחן ערוך כפי מה שיוכל.
Now let him honor the Sabbath with clean clothing and a set table as best he can.

ויאכל שלש סעודות.
And he should eat three meals.

אל ידבר שום דבר בחפציו הצריכים לו, אך בחפצי-שמים.
Let him not speak a word of his desires that he needs, but only the desires of Heaven.

Sefer HaYirah   ספר היראה

חשבונות שעברו, מותר.
Prior reckonings are permitted.

ואל ירבה שיחה אם לא בדברי תורה ויראת שמים, כי אף שאלת שלום התירו בקושי.
Let him not increase conversation if it is not words of Torah and fear of Heaven, for even peaceful requests permit difficulty.

ואל יפסיע פסיעה גסה אם לא ללכת לדבר מצווה, ולא שום טורח אל יעשה.
Let him not march with hasty steps if not to go to do a mitzvah, and no manner of preparation let him not do.

ואל ידבר מאוהביו שמתו ומכל עוגמת נפש.
Let him not speak of loved ones that died, or any manner of grief of the soul.

כללו של דבר, נקרא יום ענג ומנוחה.
The rule of the matter - the Sabbath is called a day of pleasure and rest.

ויוסיף מן החול על הקודש, ואל יוציא דמעה מעיניו. וישמרהו כהלכותיו על פי רבותינו עליהם השלום.
Let him add from the profane upon the holy. and let no tear come forth from his eyes. But let him keep it according to the laws taught by our Sages, may peace be upon them.

במוצאי שבת יבדיל בתפלה ועל הכוס של יין.
On Saturday evening let him make a separation

Sefer HaYirah   ספר היראה

with prayer, and over the cup of wine.

לא הבדיל בתפלה ובא לעשות צרכיו, במלאכה האסורה בשבת, קדם שהבדיל, יברך, ברוך אתה ה', אלוהינ"ו מלך העולם, המבדיל בין קודש לחול, ויעשה צרכיו.

If he **did not** separate the Sabbath from the weekday with a prayer, and he wants to do other weekday work. He must say this blessing. Let him bless as follows - You are blessed, ETERNAL our God, ruler of the universe, who separates between sacred and profane. Then he may do any weekday work.

ויסדר[160] שולחנו במוצאי שבת, אף על פי שאינו צריך אלא לכזית.

Then he should set his table on Saturday night, even though he only needs to eat as much as an olive.

וילווה המלכה בשירות ותשבחות.

Then he should send out the King with song and praise.

ובערב יום טוב ינהג בעצמו כמו שאמרנו בערב שבת.

And on festival eve, let him conduct himself as we have said on Sabbath eve.

---

[160] שבת קיט ב

Sefer HaYirah   ספר הירא֭ה

Holidays חגים

כללו של דבר - לכל זמן בעת שמחה, בפורים, ירבה בשמחה ובמשתה.

The rule of the matter - for every time at a season of rejoicing, rejoice. At Purim let him increase joy and drinking.

אך שיהא לבו לשמים, שלא יצא מפיו דבר ערווה ונבול פה.

But his heart should be directed to Heaven, so that no word of immorality or obscenity comes out of his mouth.

בעת עצב - עצב.

And in a season of sorrow, be sorrowful.

משנכנס[161] אב, ממעטים בשמחה.

When the Hebrew month of **Av** enters, joy decreases.

משנכנס אלול עד מוצאי יום הכיפורים, יהא חרד וירא מאימת הדין.

When the Hebrew month of **Elul** enters, until the night after the **Yom Kippur** [Day of Atonement], be trembling and fearful from being scared of the Judgment.

תמיד בכל חודש, יום אחד או יותר ישב בתענית, או לכל הפחות יאכל לחם ומים.

---

[161] תענית כו ב

Sefer HaYirah ספר היראה

In every month, one should always sit one or more days in fasting or at least eating only bread and water.

ואותו יום יהיה בבכי ובמספד. בכי, זה הבוכה בדמעות. ומספד, כאדם הסופד על מתו, מספר מעשיו ואומר, אוי לי שעשיתי חטא פלוני, אוי לי, כמה חייבתי נפשי למלכו של עולם.

On that day he should sit in crying and lamentation. Crying - This is the one who cries with tears. Lamentation - Like a man who mourns his death, recounting his deeds and saying - Woe to me, That I have done such-and-such sin, Woe to me, that I am liable for the death-penalty unto the Eternal King.

וזוהי התשובה המעולה שנאמרה על ידי יואל הנביא - וקרעו[162] לבבכם ואל בגדיכם ושובו אל ה' בצום ובבכי ובמספד.

But this is the exalted repentance said by Yoel the prophet - Now tear your hearts, not your clothes and turn back to the Lord. with fasting, with crying, and with lamenting.

ויתהה על עוונות נעוריו שעשה ואל ישוב לעשות עוד.

Let him gaze upon the sins of his youth that he has done and never return to them any more.

ויתהה על עונותיו הגלויים לו כהוויתם, ויהיה מודה ועוזב ולא טובל ושרץ בידו.

And every day he confesses over his sins that

---

[162] יואל ב יג

Sefer HaYirah ספר היראה

are known to him as they stand, so he should be gratefully acknowledging and letting go of them, and not like one who enters a ritual bath with a lizard in his hand.

ויתפלל בכל יום כפי צחות לשונו על כל חולי בני ישראל שיתרפאו.

Let him pray every day, as beautifully as he can for all of the ill of the holy nation, that they may be healed.

ועל הבריאים שלא יחלו ושינצלו מכל נזק.

And for all the healthy ones that they may not fall ill, and that they may be saved from all damage.

ושיציל הקדוש ברוך הוא את בני ישראל מכל גויים, ומרוחות רעות, ומדקדוקי עניות, ומכל מיני פורענויות המתרגשות ובאות לעולם.

And that the Holy One, Blessed be He, may save his people Israel from all enemies and from evil spirits and from the sufferings of poverty and from all kinds of divine punishments which rush to enter the world.

ושיתיר את כל אסירי עמו.

and that He may free all the captives of His people of Israel.

ושיתיר את כל חבלי היולדות.

and that He may untie the bonds of the women in the throes of birth.

Sefer HaYirah ספר היראה

ושישיב ליראתו כל האנוסים ביד גויים.
and that He may bring back to the fear of Him all those forcibly seized by the Nations.

ועל חשוכי בנים שייתן להם זרע טוב וכשר.
And for all those lacking children that He may give them good and kosher children.

ועל אותם שיש להם בנים שיחיו ביראת השם.
And for those that have them, that they may live in fear of the God.

ועל כולם שישמור הקדוש ברוך הוא שארית תורתו, וינקום את נקמתם במהרה בימינו.
And for all of them, that the Holy One, Blessed be He, may guard the remnant of His people. And that He may execute their judgment speedily and in our days.

ועל עם הקודש שישובו בתשובה שלמה, ויקבלם ויחזירם בתשובה שלמה לפניו.
And for the holy people, let them return in complete repentance, that he may receive them and take them back in complete repentance before Him.

ויקרא בכל יום בפרשת - **ועתה**[163] **ישראל**. שכולה יראת שמים, למען יזכור תמיד את הבורא ולא יחטא.
Every day one should read the Torah portion beginning - **And now Israel, what does the Lord require of you**. For all of it is fear of

---

[163] דברים י יב

Sefer HaYirah   ספר היראה

God, so that he may always remember the Creator and that he may not sin.

www.ingramcontent.com/pod-product-compliance
Lightning Source LLC
Chambersburg PA
CBHW070154080526
44586CB00015B/1981